Streetwise

atlas of CARDIFF
Barry & Penarth

G000136415

Key to street plans

Plans drawn at a scale of 4 inches to 1 mile

M4	Motorway
A48	A road (Trunk road)
A48	Dual carriageway
B4281	B road
	Through road
- - - - -	Track/Footpath
—··—··—	County boundary
—···—···—	Municipal boundary
▬▬■▬▬	Railway
░░░	Woods and forest

P	Car parks (major)
☉ ✝ ✡	Places of worship
🏠 🍺	Hotel/Public house
⛽ 🚕	Petrol station/Taxi rank
🔔	Police station
✉	Post Office
Ⓜ 🎭	Theatre/Museum
🚻	Toilet facility
⊕	Health centre/Clinic
🚐 ⛺	Caravan/camping sites

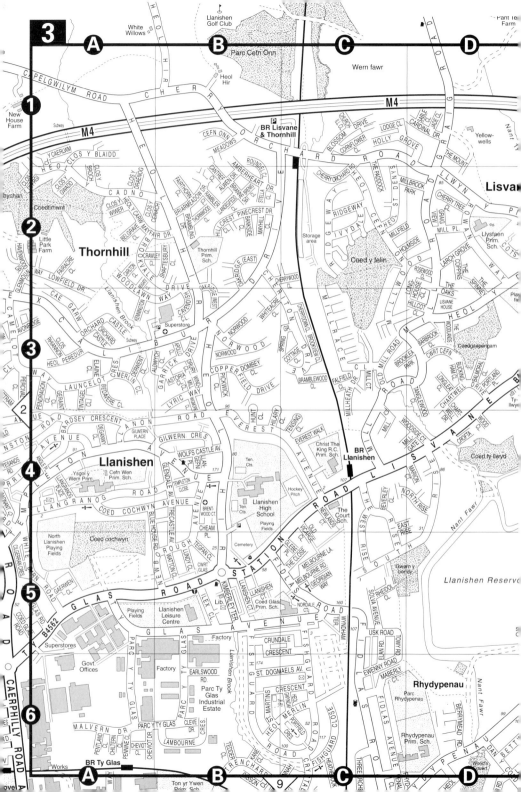

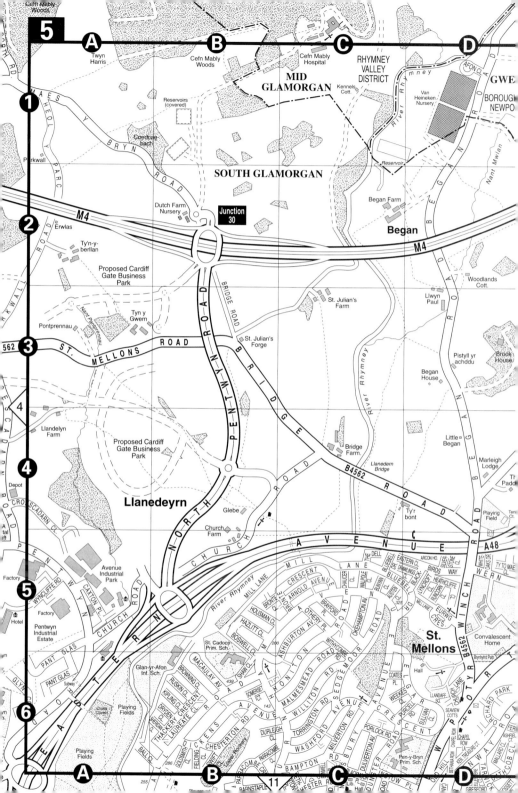

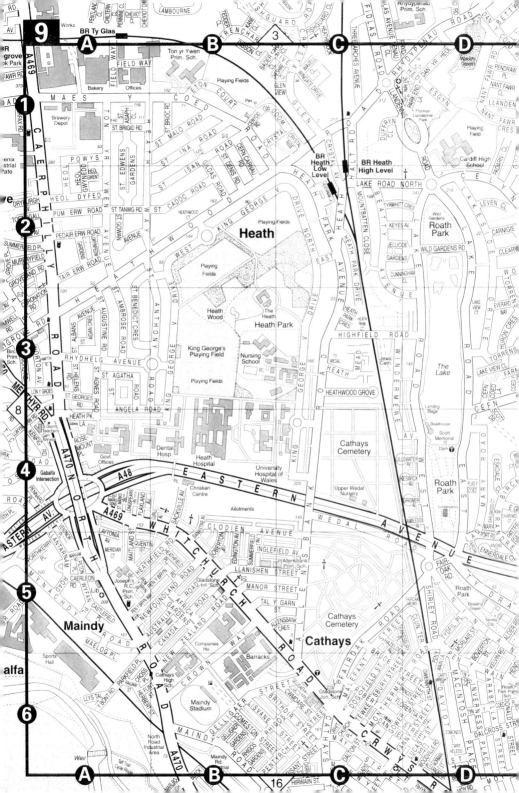

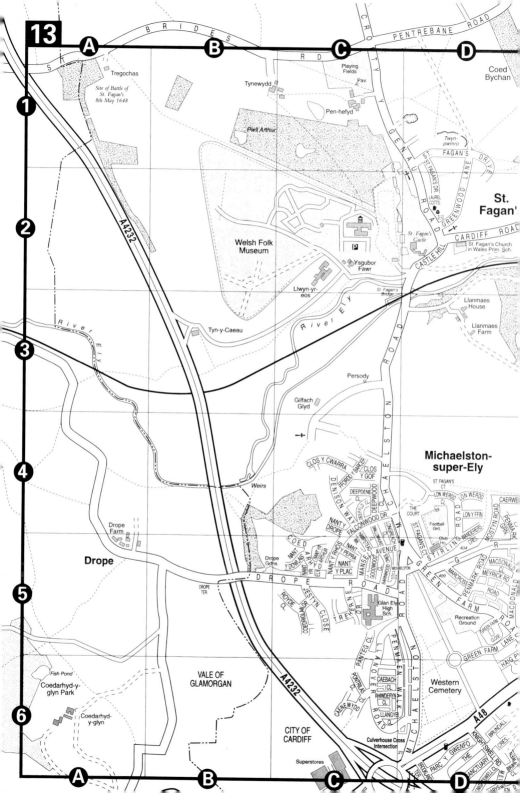

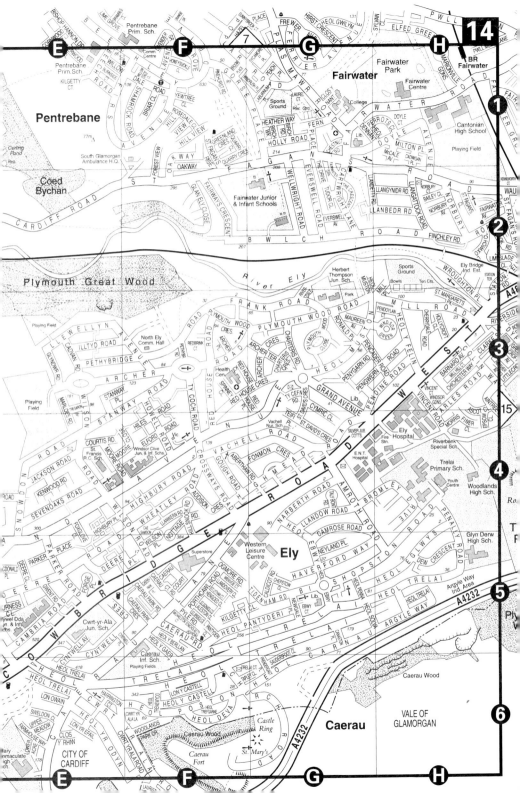

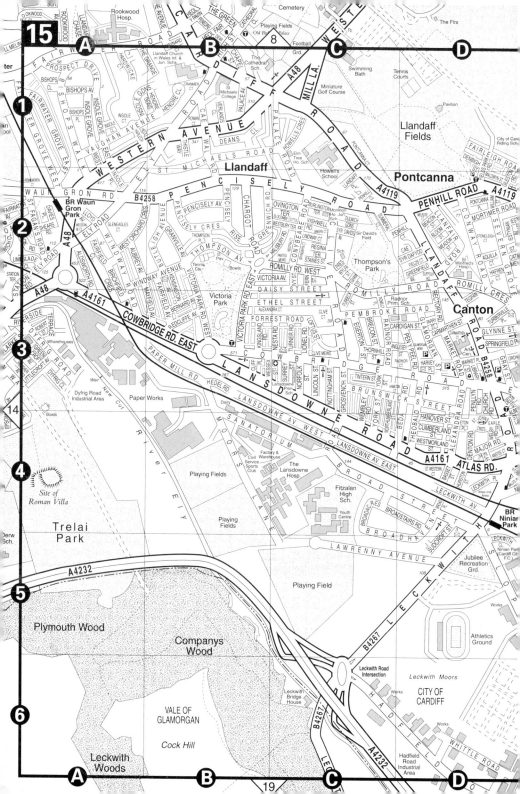

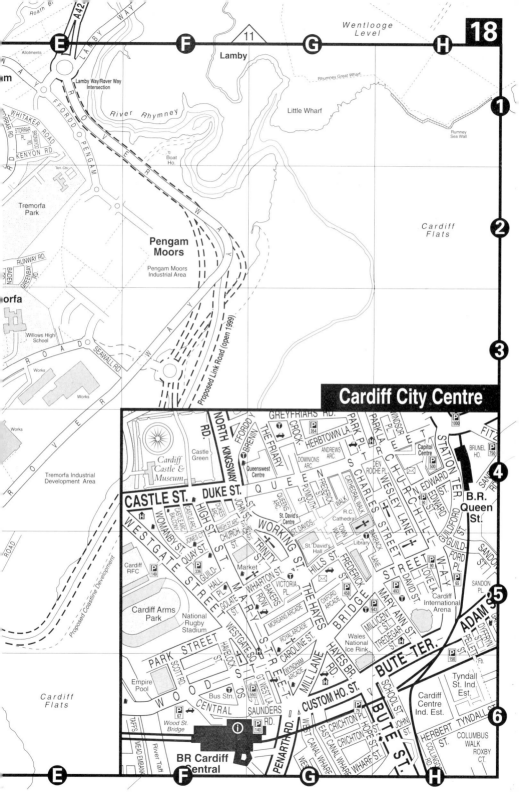

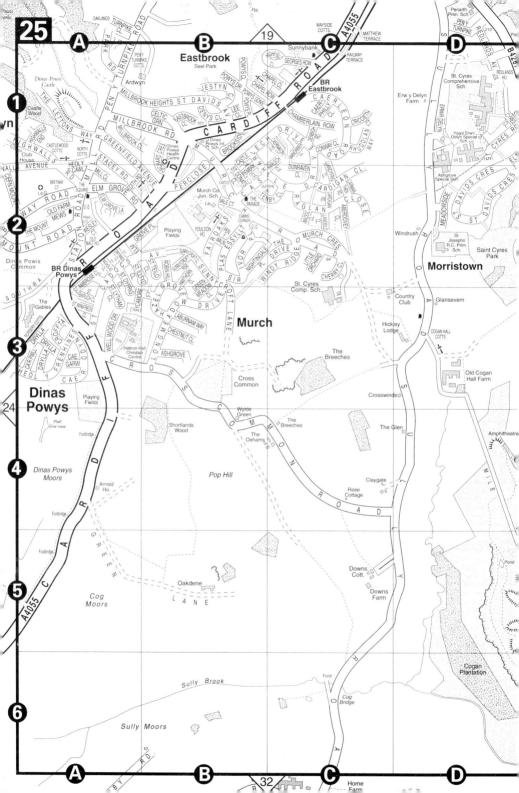

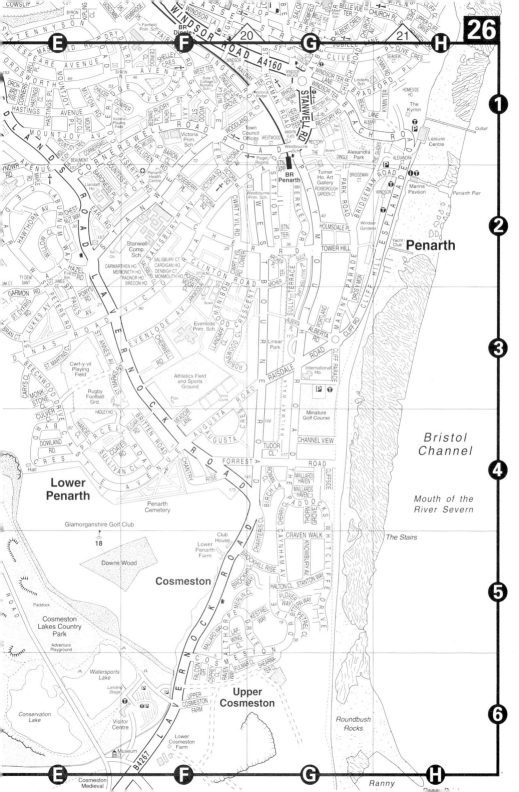

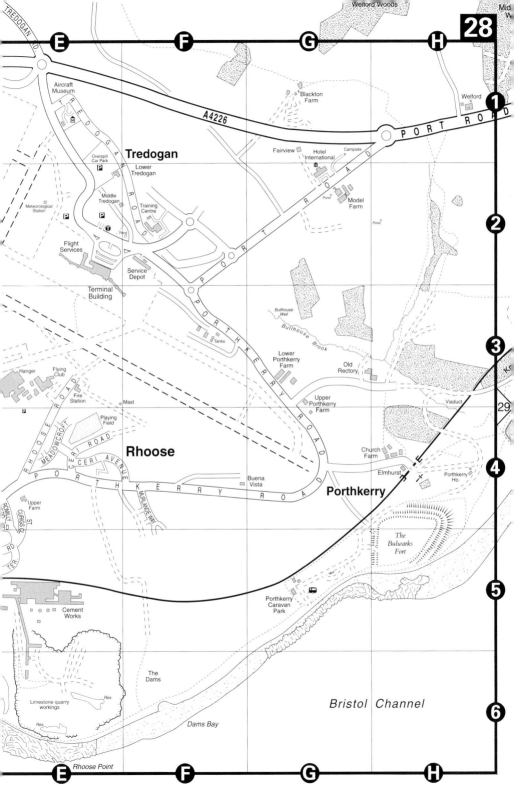

Welford Woods

Mid
W

E F G H

1

Welford

A4226

PORT ROAD

Aircraft
Museum

Blackton
Farm

Tredogan

Overspill
Car Park

Fairview

Hotel
International

Campsite

2

Lower
Tredogan

Pond

Model
Farm

Middle
Tredogan

Training
Centre

Meteorological
Station

Pond

Pond

Flight
Services

Bullhouse
Well

Service
Depot

Bullhouse Brook

3

Terminal
Building

Lower
Porthkerry
Farm

Old
Rectory

Tanks

Upper
Porthkerry
Farm

K

Hanger

Flying
Club

Viaduct

29

Fire
Station

Mast

Church
Farm

Playing
Field

Rhoose

Elmhurst

Porthkerry
Ho.

4

MEADOWCROFT

Buena
Vista

Porthkerry

Upper
Farm

The
Bulwarks
Fort

CURIGS CL

5

Cement
Works

Porthkerry
Caravan
Park

Limestone quarry
workings

Res.

The
Dams

Res.

Bristol Channel

6

Dams Bay

E Rhoose Point F G H

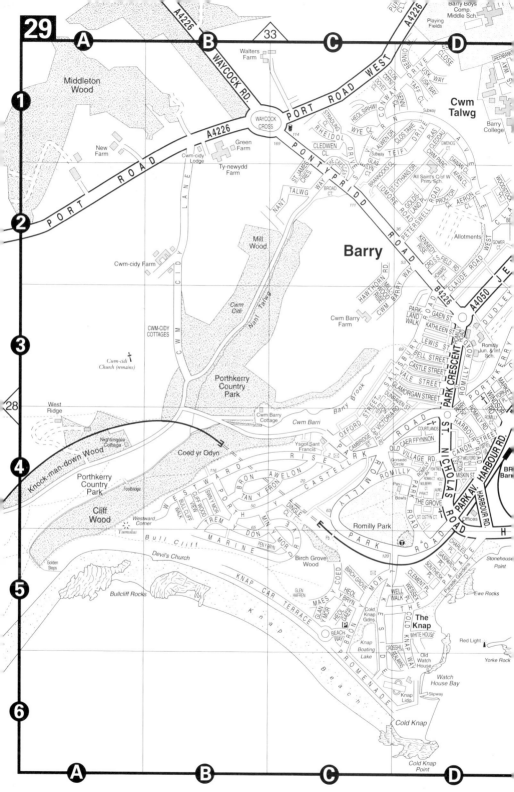

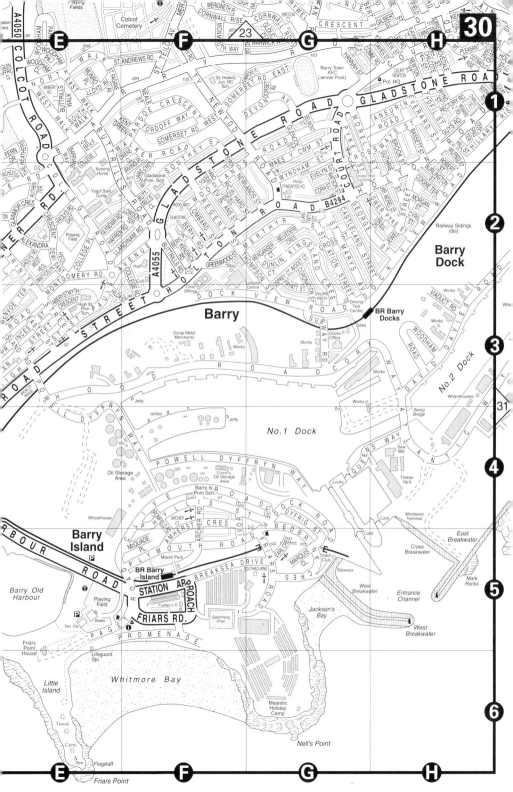

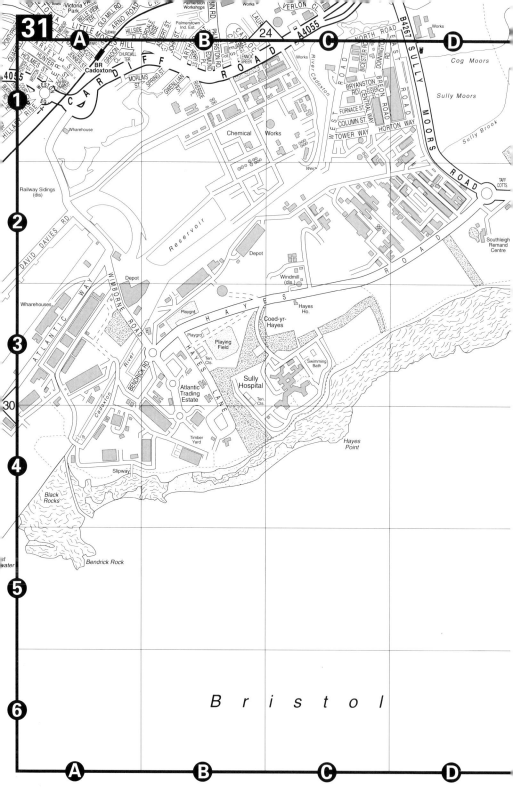

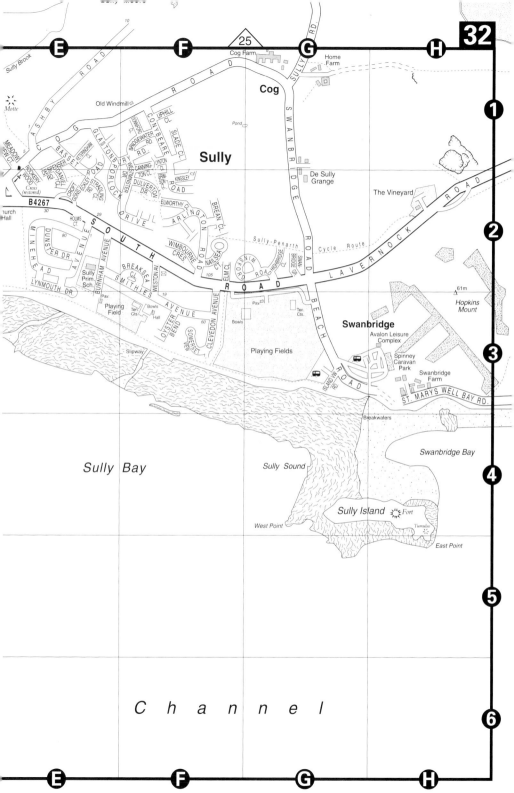

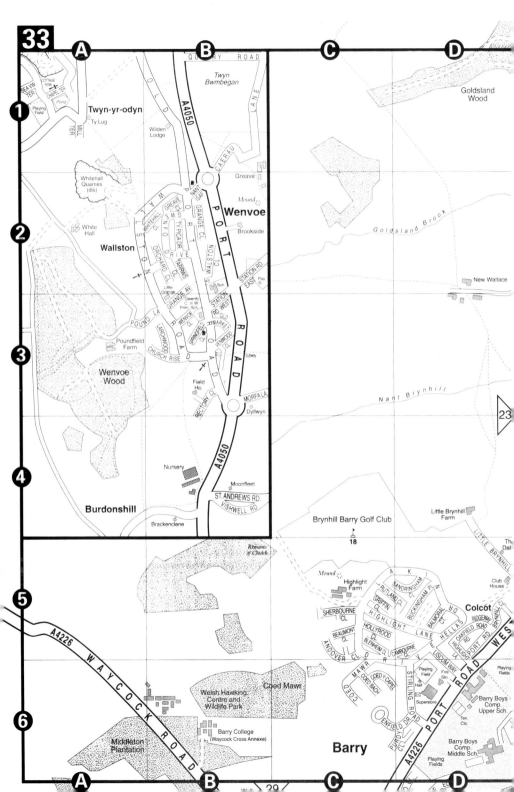

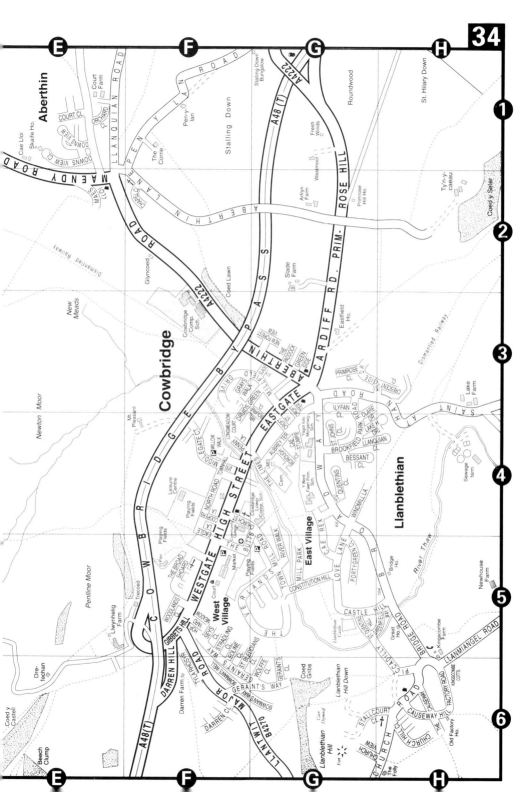

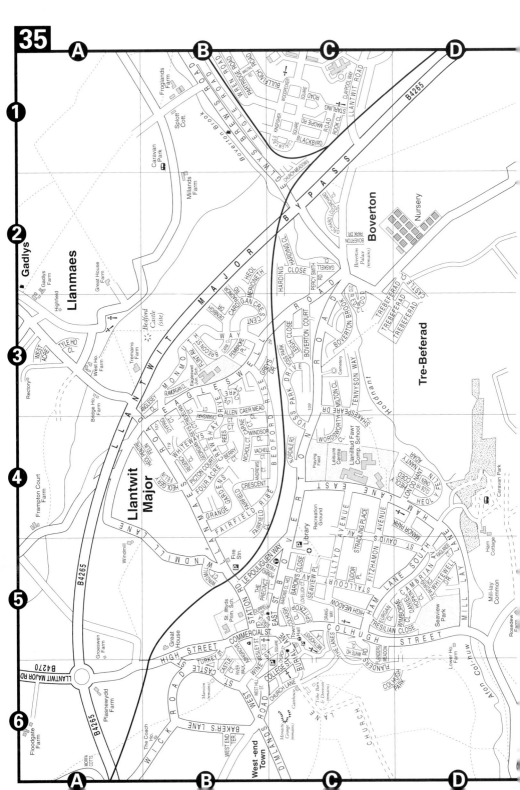

INDEX

Abbreviations used

Av.	Avenue	Cres.	Crescent	Ho.	House	Prim.	Primary
App.	Approach	Dis.	Disused	Ind.	Industrial	Rec.	Recreation
Br.	Bridge	Dr.	Drive	Inf.	Infant	Rd.	Road
Bldgs.	Buildings	E.	East	Junc.	Junction	Sch.	School
Bus.	Business	Ent.	Enterprise	La.	Lane	S.	South
Cara.	Caravan	Est.	Estate	Lib.	Library	Sq.	Square
Cem.	Cemetery	Fb.	Footbridge	Lit.	Little	Stn.	Station
Cl.	Close	Gdns.	Gardens	Mt.	Mount	St.	Street
Comm.	Community	Grn.	Green	N.	North	Ter.	Terrace
Comp.	Comprehensive	Grd.	Ground	Pk.	Park	Up.	Upper
Cott(s).	Cottage(s)	Gr.	Grove	Pav.	Pavilion	Wlk.	Walk
Ct.	Court	Hosp.	Hospital	Pl.	Place	W.	West

Use of this Index

1. An alphabetical order is followed.

2. Each street name is followed by a map reference giving a page number and coordinates: Abbey Close 1 A2.

3. Where a street runs across more than one page the reference number is given: Ball Road 5 B6-11 B2.

4. Where a street name appears more than once the reference is given: Cherrydown Close 3 C2/C3.

5. House numbers along streets are shown: 250.

A

Abbey Close 1 A2
Aber Street 16 G6
Aberbran Road.................8 G5
Abercynon Street.................20 G1
Aberdaron Road.................11 D2
Aberdore Road.................8 G5
Aberdovey Close.................25 C2
Aberdovey Street 17 C4
Aberdulais Crescent 8 F4
Aberdulais Road.................8 F5
Abergele Close.................11 D1
Abergele Road 11 D2
Abernethy Close 6 G6
Aberporth Road.................8 F4
Aberteifi Close 8 H5
Aberteifi Crescent 8 H5
Aberthaw Road (Ely) ...14 F4
Aberthaw Road (Rhoose)...27 A5
Aberthin Lane.................34 F2
Aberthin Road.................34 G3
Aberystwyth Crescent ...30 E3
Aberystwyth Street.................17 C4
Abingdon Street 23 D6
Adam Street.................17 A4/18 H5
Adams Court.................17 A3
Adamsdown Lane.................17 A4
Adamsdown Place 17 B4
Adamsdown Square.................17 A3
Addison Crescent 14 F4
Adelaide Place.................20 H1
Adelaide Street.................21 A1
Adeline Street 17 B3
Adenfield Way.................27 B4
Admirals Landing.................17 A5
Ael y Bryn (Llanederyrn)...10 F3
Ael y Bryn (Radyr).................1 A6
Aeron Close.................29 D2
Afan Close.................29 D2
Afon Close 5 D1
Africa Gardens.................9 B5
Agate Street.................17 B3
Agincourt Road.................10 F6
Agnes Street.................20 F6
Aintree Drive 14 H3
Albany Court 26 G1
Albany Road.................16 H1-17 B1
Albert Crescent 20 H6
Albert Road 26 G1
Albert Street (Barry).................3 D3
Albert Street (Riverside)......16 E3
Albert Street Lane 15 D3
Albert Walk 16 E4
Alberta Place.................26 G3
Alberta Road.................26 G3
Alder Road.................9 D5

Alderbrook 4 F4
Alderwood Close 6 E6
Aldsworth Road.................15 A2
Aldwych Close.................3 B3
Alexander Street 9 C6
Alexandra Court (Canton) ...15 B3
Alexandra Court (Penarth)...26 H1
Alexandra Crescent 30 E2
Alexandra Road 15 D4
Alfred Street.................10 E6
Alfreda Court 8 E3
Alfreda Road.................8 E3
Alfreds Terrace 1 A2
Alice Street 16 H6
Allan Durst Close.................7 C4
Allen Court (Llantwit Major)..35 B3
Allens Court (Cyncoed) 10 E1
Allensbank Crescent 9 C5
Allensbank Road 9 C3-C5
Allerton Street.................16 F5
Alltmawr Road.................10 E1
Alltwen 2 E5
Alma Road.................10 E6
Almond Drive.................4 H4
Althorpe Drive.................26 F5
Alwen Drive (Barry) 29 C1
Alwen Drive (Thornhill) 3 B2
Amber Close.................4 H4
Ambergate Drive 4 H4
Amberheart Drive 3 B2
Amberley Close.................4 H4
Amberwood Close.................4 H4
Amblecote Close.................4 H4
Ambleside Avenue 9 D4
Ambrook Close.................4 H4
Amesbury Road.................10 F6
Amethyst Road.................7 C6
Amherst Crescent 30 F5
Amherst Street.................20 G1
Amroth Court.................23 C5
Amroth Road.................14 G4
Amyas Close 16 E5
Anchor Court.................17 A5
Anchor Way 20 F5
Anderson Place.................17 B3
Andover Close.................33 C5
Andrew Road.................20 E5
Andrews Arcade.................18 G4
Andrews Court.................35 B4
Andrews Road.................8 E5
Aneurin Road.................30 H1
Angelina Street.................16 H5
Angle Close 23 B5
Angle Place 3 A4
Anglesey Close.................35 B3
Anglesey Street.................15 C3

Angus Street.................10 E6
Ann Street.................16 E3
Anson Court.................17 A5
Anstee Court 15 D4
Anton Court.................8 F2
Apollo Close 3 B3
Appledore Road 8 H4
Applewood Close 17 B4
Aquilla Court.................15 D2
Ar y Nant 23 D5
Arabella Street.................9 D6
Archer Court.................30 F4
Archer Crescent 14 G3
Archer Place (Ely).................14 F3
Archer Place (Penarth) 26 G2
Archer Road (Barry Island)..30 F5
Archer Road (Ely).................14 E3
Archer Road (Penarth) 26 F2
Archer Terrace (Ely).................14 G3
Archer Terrace (Penarth)...26 G2
Arcon House.................5 D5
Arcot Lane North.................20 G6
Arcot Street.................20 G5
Arden Way.................24 E5
Ardwyn.................2 E5
Argae Lane.................24 F2-F5
Argyle Way 14 H5
Arles Road.................14 H3
Arlington Crescent 11 B1
Arlington Road.................32 F2
Arno Road.................24 E6
Arnold Avenue.................5 C5
Arnside Road.................10 E5
Arran Place 17 B1
Arran Street 17 A1
Arrol Street 17 B4
Arthur Davis Court 23 B6
Arthur Street (Adamsdown) 17 C2
Arthur Street (Cadoxton) 31 B1
Arundel Place.................16 E6
Ascot Close.................14 H3
Asgog Street.................17 B3
Ash Grove (Barry).................24 E6
Ash Grove (Penarth).................20 F5
Ash Grove (Whitchurch) 8 F1
Ash Place 7 B6
Ash Tree Close 22 H4
Ashburton Avenue.................5 C5
Ashby Road.................32 E1
Ashcroft Crescent 7 A6
Ashdene Close.................7 C5
Ashdown Close.................6 E6
Ashford Close 8 F1
Ashgrove (Llantwit Major)..35 B5
Ashgrove (Murch).................25 B3
Ashwood Court.................17 A2

Aspen Close 6 E6
Aster Close.................6 G6
Astoria Close 3 B3
Athelstan Road.................8 E3
Atlantic Place 24 E6
Atlantic Way.................30 H4-31 A3
Atlantic Wharf Close.................17 A5
Atlas Place 15 D4
Atlas Road.................15 D4
Aubrey Avenue.................15 A2
Aubrey Terrace 34 G3
Augusta Crescent 26 F4
Augusta Road.................26 F4
Augusta Street.................17 A3
Austen Close 5 C5
Australia Road.................9 B5
Avenue, The (Llandaff).........8 F6
Avenue, The (Rumney)......11 C5
Avenue, The (Whitchurch) ...8 E3
Avoca Place.................16 F5
Avocet Close 24 E6
Avon Close.................24 E6
Avondale Crescent 20 G1
Avondale Gardens 20 G1
Avondale Gardens South...20 G1
Avondale Road 20 G1
Avonmuir Road 17 D1
Avonridge 2 H3
Awbery House 30 E1
Awel Mor.................10 F4
Axbridge Crescent 11 C1
Axminster Road.................17 C1
Aylesbury Mansions 8 E1
Azalea Close.................4 F6

B

Bacton Close.................8 G5
Bacton Road.................8 G5
Baden Road.................18 E2
Bader Close.................9 B1
Bailey Close.................14 H2
Bakers Court 15 C2
Bakers Lane 35 B6
Bakers Row.................18 G5
Bala Road.................8 F5
Balaclava Road.................10 E6
Baldwin Close.................7 C3
Ball Close 5 A6
Ball Lane 5 A6
Ball Road 5 B6-11 B2
Balmoral Close.................3 D3
Balmoral Court 33 D5
Bampton Road.................5 C6
Banastre Avenue.................9 B5
Bangor Street 10 E6
Bankside Close 3 B2
Banwell Place.................5 C6

Barber Close 10 G6
Barberry Rise.................20 E6
Barbrook Close.................3 D3
Bardsey Crescent.................3 A4
Bargoed Street.................16 G6
Barmouth Road 11 B4
Barnard Avenue 14 H3
Barnstaple Road.................11 B1
Barnwood Crescent 13 C5
Baron Court 26 F1
Baron Road.................26 E2
Baroness Place 26 E2
Barons Close.................35 C5
Barons Close House.................35 C5
Barons Court 20 F5
Barons Court Road.................10 F5
Barrack Lane.................18 G5
Barrington Road.................8 G3
Barry Docks Link Road
.................23 D3-24 G5
Barry Road (Barry) ...23 D6-30 E1
Barry Road (Llandough)...20 E5
Basil Place.................16 H1
Bassaleg Close.................6 F6
Bassett Road.................32 E1
Bassett Street (Barry)...30 H1
Bassett Street (Canton) ...15 D4
Bastian Close 24 E6
Batchelor Road 8 H5
Bayside Road.................17 B4
Baywatch Close 7 D5
Beach Lane.................26 G1
Beach Road (Penarth) 20 G1
Beach Road (Sully).................32 G3
Beachway.................29 C5
Beacon Street 15 D2
Beale Close.................7 D5
Beatrice Road (Barry) 30 H1
Beatrice Road (Whitchurch)..8 F3
Beatty Avenue 9 C2
Beatty Close 23 C4
Beatty Court.................17 A5
Beauchamp Street.................16 F4
Beaufort Court 17 A5
Beaumaris Road.................11 B4
Beaumont Close.................33 C5
Beaumont Court 26 E1
Beaumont Way.................17 B3
Beauville Lane.................24 H1
Beda Road.................15 D4
Bedavere Close.................3 A3
Bedford Place 17 A2
Bedford Rise.................9 C5
Bedford Street.................16 H2/17 A2
Bedlington Terrace.................29 D2
Bedwas Close.................6 F6

Bedwas Place 26 F1
Bedwas Street 16 F6
Beech Court 1 C3
Beech Ho. (Hollybush Est.)...1 A6
Beech Road 14 E1
Beech Tree Close 22 H4
Beecher Avenue 20 G2
Beechley Drive 7 A6/14 F1
Beechwood Drive 26 E3
Beechwood Road 1 A1
Began Road 5 D1-D4
Belgrave Close 3 A2
Belgrave Court 16 F4
Bell Street 29 D3
Belle Vue Close 20 H6
Belle Vue Crescent 8 E3
Belle Vue Terrace (Barry) ..24 E6
Belle Vue Terrace (Penarth)20 H6
Belmont Street 30 G1
Belmont Walk 17 A6
Belvedere Crescent 30 G2
Bendrick Road 31 A3
Beresford Lane 17 C1
Beresford Road 17 C1
Berkeley Court 10 E1
Berkley Drive 26 G2
Bernard Avenue 15 B3
Bernio Close 29 D1
Berry Court 35 B5
Berry Place 7 B5
Berrymead Road 3 D6
Berthwin Street 16 E2
Bertram Street 17 C2
Beryl Place 30 F2
Beryl Road 30 F2
Bessant Close 34 G4
Bessborough Drive 16 E6
Bessemer Close 19 D1
Bessemer Road 16 E6
Bethania Row 5 D6
Bettws y Coed Road 3 D6-4 E6
Beulah Road 2 G6
Beverley Close 3 C4
Beverley Street 23 D6
Bicester Road 31 C1
Bideford Road 11 C2
Birch Court 1 B3
Birch Grove 29 C5
Birch Hill 1 B4
Birch Lane 26 G4
Birch Walk 14 G1
Birchfield Crescent 15 A2
Birchgrove Road 8 H3
Birchwood Gardens 8 H4
Birchwood Lane 10 E4
Birchwood Park 8 H4
Birchwood Road 9 D4-10 E4
Bishop Hannon Drive 7 A6
Bishop Street 16 F6
Bishops Avenue 15 A1
Bishops Close (Llandaff) ...15 A1
Bishops Close (Whitchurch) ..8 F3
Bishops Place (Llandaff) ...15 A1
Bishops Place (Whitchurch) ..8 F3
Bishops Road 8 E3
Bishops Walk 15 A1
Bishopston Road 14 G5
Bittern Way 26 G5
Black Oak Court 4 E4
Black Oak Road 4 E5
Blackbird Road 35 C1
Blackbirds Way 5 D5
Blackmoor Place 5 C6
Blackstone Street 16 E4
Blackweir Cottages 16 F1
Blackweir Terrace 16 F1
Blackwell Close 23 D6
Blaen y Coed (Radyr) 22 H4
Blaen y Coed (Rhiwbina) 2 H5
Blaenavon Close 6 F6
Blaenclydach Place 16 G1
Blaenclydach Street 16 G1

Blagdon Close 11 B2
Blaina Close 6 F6
Blake Court 17 A5
Blanche Street 17 C1
Blandings Court 10 E1
Blandon Way 8 F3
Blanthorn Court 8 E1
Blenheim Close 33 C5
Blenheim Road 10 F6
Blethin Close 7 D4
Bloom Street 15 D2
Blosse Road 8 E5
Blossom Drive 3 C1
Blue House Road 3 A4
Bluebell Drive 5 C5
Blyth Close 23 C4
Bodnant Close 12 E1
Boleyn Walk 10 E5
Boncath Road 8 F5
Bonvilston House 23 C5
Booker Street 17 C2
Boon Close 23 D5
Borough Avenue 23 A5
Borough Close 34 G4
Borrowdale Close 10 E4
Borth Road 11 D2
Boswell Close 5 B5
Boulevard de Nantes 16 G3
Boverton Brook 35 C3
Boverton Park Drive 35 C2
Boverton Road 35 C5
Boverton Street 9 D5
Bowmans Way 34 G6
Bowmans Well 34 F6
Brachdy Lane 11 B5
Brachdy Road 11 B5
Bracken Place 7 B5
Bradenham Place 26 G1
Bradford Place 26 G1
Bradford Street 20 G1
Bradley Street 17 C2
Braeval Street 16 H1
Bramble Close 7 A6
Bramble Rise 20 E6
Bramblewood Close 3 C3
Brambling Drive 3 B2
Brandreth Road 9 D4-10 E5
Brangwyn Close 20 F6
Branksome House 16 G4
Brannocks Close 29 C2
Branwen Close 13 D6
Braunton Avenue 11 B1
Braunton Crescent 11 B1
Brayford Place 5 C5
Breaksea Close 32 F2
Breaksea Drive 30 F5
Brean Close 32 F2
Brecon Court 23 C6
Brecon House 26 F2
Brecon Street (Canton) 15 C3
Brecon Street (Llantwit Major)
..................................35 B3
Brendon Close 11 C1
Brenig Close 3 B2
Brentwood Court 3 B4
Breon Road 31 C1
Briardene Avenue 3 B2
Briar Close 14 F1
Briarmeadow Drive 3 B2
Briarwood Drive 4 F6
Bridge Road (Cowbridge) ..34 H5
Bridge Road (Llandaff) 8 E5
Bridge Road (Llanederyrn)...5 B3
Bridge Street (Barry) 23 D6
Bridge Street (Centre) 18 G5
Bridge Street (Llandaff) 8 F6
Bridge Street (Penarth) 20 F6
Bridgeman Court 26 G2
Bridgeman Road 26 G2
Bridgewater Road (Llanrumney)
..................................11 C1
Bridgewater Road (Sully) ..32 F1
Brigantine Place 17 A5

Brindley Road 19 D1
Britannia Road 21 A1
Brithdir Street 9 C6
British Legion Drive 11 A3
Britten Road 26 F4
Britway Court 25 A2
Britway Road 25 A2
Broad Court 29 C2
Broad Place 15 D4
Broad Shoard, The 34 F5
Broad Sreet (Barry) 30 E3
Broad Street (Canton) 15 C4
Broad Street (Gwent) 12 H4
Broad Street Parade 30 E3
Broadacres 15 C4
Broadcastle Road 8 F1
Broadhaven 15 C4
Broadlands Court 6 E6
Broadlands House 16 E6
Broadstairs Road 15 C4
Broadway (Cowbridge) 34 H5
Broadway (Roath) 17 B2
Broadwell Close 12 F1
Brock Street 24 E6
Brockhampton Road 6 E6
Brockhill Rise 26 G5
Brockhill Way 26 F5
Bromfield Place 20 H6
Bromfield Street 20 G1
Bromley Drive 14 G4
Bromsgrove Street 20 F1
Bron Awelon 29 B4
Bron Felin 2 H3
Bron y Mor 29 C5
Bronte Close 5 B5
Bronte Crescent 5 C5
Bronwydd Avenue 10 E5
Bronwydd Close 10 F5
Bronwydd Road 18 E1
Brook Road (Fairwater) 15 A2
Brook Road (Whitchurch) 8 F3
Brook Street (Barry) 30 H1
Brook Street (Riverside) 16 F4
Brookfield Avenue 24 E5
Brookfield Drive 12 E1
Brooklands Terrace 13 D6
Brooklea Park 3 C3
Brooklyn Close 2 F4
Brookside 25 B1
Brookside Close 8 H2
Brookvale Drive 3 A2
Brookview Close 3 C3
Broom Place 14 F1
Broomfield Road 30 F4
Broughton Place 23 C5
Browning Close 5 B6
Bruce Knight Close 7 D5
Bruce Street 9 C6
Brundall Crescent 13 D6
Brunel Close 24 F5
Brunel House 16 H3
Brunel Street 16 F4
Brunswick Street 15 C3
Bruton Place 8 F6
Bryanston Road 31 C1
Brydges Place 16 G1
Bryn Adar 2 G5
Bryn Bach 2 G5
Bryn Castell 1 A6
Bryn Celyn 4 H6
Bryn Celyn Road 10 H1
Bryn Derwyn 1 A6/22 H3/H4
Bryn Glas 2 H3
Bryn Golwg 1 A6
Bryn Haidd 4 H6
Bryn Heulog (Pentwyn) 4 H6
Bryn Heulog (Whitchurch) 8 F3
Bryn Pinwydden 4 G5
Bryn Rhosyn 22 H3
Bryn y Nant 10 H2
Brynawelon Road 4 E5
Brynbala Way 11 D2-12 E2

Bryncoed 22 H3
Bryncyn 4 G5
Brynderwen Close 10 E2
Brynfedw 10 F1/G2
Bryngwyn Court 15 C2
Bryngwyn Road 4 E6
Brynhill 10 E1
Brynhill Close 33 D5
Brynhyfryd 1 A6
Brynmawr Close 6 G6
Brynnau Road 1 A1
Brynteg 2 F4
Brynteg Close 10 E3
Bryntirion 2 G5
Buckingham Close 3 D3
Buckingham Place 33 D5
Buckley Close 7 C4
Bull Cliff Walk 29 B4
Bullfinch Road 35 C1
Bulrush Close 12 G1
Bunyan Close 5 C5
Burges Place 16 E6
Burial Lane 35 C6
Burlington Street 30 H2
Burlington Terrace 15 C2
Burnaby Street 17 C3
Burne Jones Close 7 D5
Burnham Avenue (Llanrumney)
..........................5 C5-11 C1
Burnham Avenue (Sully) ..32 E2
Burnham Court 11 C1
Burns Crescent 23 B5
Burnside Court 14 E1
Burt Street 20 H2
Bute Crescent 21 A1
Bute Esplanade 21 A2
Bute Lane 26 F1
Bute Place 21 A1
Bute Street (Canton) 16 H5-21 A1
Bute Street (Tongwynlais) ...1 B4
Butetown Link Road 20 G3
Butleigh Avenue 15 B2
Butt Lee Court 30 F2
Buttrills Close 30 F2
Buttrills Road 30 E1/F2
Buttrills Walk 30 E1
Butts, The 34 F5
Bwlch Road 14 G2
Byrd Crescent 26 E4
Byron Court 20 F6
Byron Place 26 F1
Byron Street (Barry) 30 F1
Byron Street (Roath) 17 A2
C
Ca'r Pwll 25 A3
Cadnant Close 2 H4
Cadoc Crescent 24 E6
Cadvan Road 14 E3
Cadwgan Place 14 H1
Cae Garw (Murch) 25 A3
Cae Garw (Thornhill) 3 A3
Cae Glas 23 D6
Cae Glas Avenue 11 B4
Cae Glas Road 11 B4
Cae Leon 23 B4
Cae Lewis 1 B4
Cae Maen 8 H3
Cae Mawr Road 2 H5
Cae Rex 34 G5
Cae Samson 14 F4
Cae Stumpie 34 G4
Cae Syr Dafydd 15 D2
Cae Tymawr 7 D3
Cae Yorath 8 G2
Cae'r Odyn 25 A3
Caebach Close 13 C6
Caedelyn Road 8 F1
Caegwyn Road 8 G3-H2
Caenewydd Close 13 C6
Caer Castell Place 11 C2
Caer Ffynnon 29 D4
Caer Graig 1 A6-22 H3
Caer Mead Close 35 B3

Caer Wenallt 2 E5
Caerau Court 14 F5
Caerau Court Road 14 F5
Caerau Lane (Caerau) 14 E6
Caerau Lane (Wenvoe) 33 B1
Caerau Park Crescent 14 F5
Caerau Park Place 14 F5
Caerau Park Road 14 F5
Caerau Road 14 F5
Caercady Close 10 E3
Caerleon Close 6 F6
Caerleon Road (Maindy) 9 A5
Caerleon Road (Murch) 25 C1
Caernarvon Close 25 C1
Caernarvon Way 11 D2
Caerphilly Close 25 C1
Caerphilly Road 2 H6-9 A3
Caerwent Road 13 D4
Caewal Road 15 B1
Cairnmuir Road 17 D2
Caldicot Road 14 G5
Caldy Close 23 C5
Caldy Road 8 E4
Cambourne Avenue 8 E2
Cambourne Close 33 D5
Cambria Road 14 E5
Cambrian Avenue 35 D5
Cambridge Street (Barry) ...29 C4
Cambridge Street (Grangetown)
..................................20 G1
Camellia Court 7 C5
Camelot Way 2 H3
Cameron Street 17 C2
Camms Corner 25 B2
Campbell Drive 20 G3
Campion Place 7 B5
Camrose Court 23 C5
Camrose Road 14 G4
Canada Road 9 B5
Canal Parade 16 H5
Canaston Place 14 G5
Cannington Avenue 11 B1
Cannington Close 32 F1
Canon Street 20 G1
Canopus Close 11 D1
Canton Court 16 E4
Cantref Close 3 B2
Capelgwilym Road 2 H1-3 A1
Caple Road 29 C4
Caradoc Avenue 23 C6
Caradog Close 6 G5
Caraway Close 6 G5
Cardiff Road (Cowbridge) ..34 G3
Cardiff Road (Llandaff)
..........................8 F6-15 C1
Cardiff Road (Llandough - Dinas
Powys) 19 D6-24 H6
Cardiff Road (St. Fagan's)
..................................13 D1-14 E1
Cardiff Road (Taff's Well) 1 A2
Cardigan Close 25 C2
Cardigan Crescent 35 B3
Cardigan House 26 F2
Cardigan Road 25 C2
Cardigan Street 15 D3
Cardinal Drive 3 D1
Carew Close 23 B6
Cargo Road 21 B2
Carisbrooke Way 10 E4
Carlisle Street 17 B3
Carlton Close 3 A2
Carmarthen Close (Barry) ..23 B6
Carmarthen Close (Llantwit
Major) 35 B3
Carmarthen Court 15 D3
Carmarthen House 26 F2
Carmarthen Road 25 C2
Carmarthen Street 15 D3
Carne Court 35 B4
Carnegie Drive 19 C5
Caroline Street 18 G6
Carter Place 7 C6
Cartwright Court 9 D6

Cartwright Lane 14 G2
Carys Close (Caerau) 13 D6
Carys Close (Penarth) 26 F3
Caspian Close 12 F1
Castell Coch View 1 B4
Castle Arcade 18 F4
Castle Arcade Balcony 18 F4
Castle Avenue (Penarth) 26 E4
Castle Avenue (Rumney) 10 H5
Castle Close (Dinas Powys)25 B1
Castle Close (Llantwit Major)
....35 D2
Castle Court..........................35 B6
Castle Crescent 10 H5
Castle Drive 25 B2
Castle Hill (Cowbridge) 34 H6
Castle Hill (St. Fagan's) 13 D2
Castle Lane 17 A2
Castle Rise 11 A4
Castle Road (Fonmon) 27 A2
Castle Road (Rhoose)
.....................................27 D5-28 E5
Castle Road (Tongwynlais) ...1 B3
Castle Street (Barry) 29 D3
Castle Street (Centre) 18 F4
Castle Street (Llantwit Major)
....35 B6
Castle View 1 C5
Castlefield Place 9 A5
Castleland Street 30 G2
Castleton Court 6 H5
Castlewood Cottages 25 A1
Caswell Road 11 B4
Cath Cob Close 5 D6
Cathays Terrace 9 C6-16 G1
Cathedral Close 8 F6
Cathedral Court 8 F6
Cathedral Green, The.............8 F6
Cathedral Road 16 E2
Cathedral View 8 G5
Cathedral Walk 18 G4
Catherine Drive 1 B3
Catherine Meazey Flats 20 H6
Catherine Street 16 G1
Catkin Drive 20 E6
Causeway Hill 34 H6
Causeway, The 34 H6
Cavendish Close 3 B3
Cawley Place 23 D6
Cawnpore Street 20 F6
Caxton Place 5 A5
Caynham Avenue 26 G5
Cecil Street 17 B2
Cedar Grove 7 B6
Cedar Ho. (Hollybush Est.) ...7 D1
Cedar Way 26 E2
Cefn Bychan 22 E1
Cefn Carnau Road 9 B1
Cefn Coch 22 H3
Cefn Coed Avenue 10 E3
Cefn Coed Crescent 10 E3
Cefn Coed Gardens 10 E4
Cefn Coed Lane 9 D3
Cefn Coed Road.........9 D3-10 E3
Cefn Graig 2 G5
Cefn Mably Road.....................4 E2
Cefn Mount 24 H2
Cefn Nant 2 F4
Cefn Onn Meadows 3 B1
Cefn Porth Road 4 H1
Cefn Road 8 H4
Ceiriog Close (Barry) 23 D5
Ceiriog Close (Penarth) 26 F1
Ceiriog Drive 2 E5
Celerity Drive 17 A5
Celtic Green 25 B1
Celtic Road 8 H4
Celtic Way 27 B5
Celyn Avenue 9 D2-10 E2
Celyn Grove 4 E6
Cemaes Crescent 12 E2
Cemetery Road (Barry) 30 F1
Cemetery Road (Taff's Well) .1 A2

Central Link Road.................17 A4
Central Square 18 F6
Central Way..........................31 C1
Ceri Avenue 28 E4
Ceri Road 28 E4
Chamberlain Road 8 E4
Chamberlain Row 25 C1
Chancery Lane 16 E4
Channel Close.......................27 C4
Channel View (Castleton) 6 G2
Channel View (Penarth).......26 G4
Channel View Flats 20 G3
Channel View Road 20 G2
Chantry Rise 26 F4
Chantry, The...........................7 D6
Chapel Close (Aberthin) 34 F2
Chapel Close (Dinas Powys)
....25 C1
Chapel Lane East 20 G6
Chapel Road............................1 A5
Chapel Row (Dinas Powys) 25 B1
Chapel Row (St. Mellons) 5 D6
Chapel Row Lane 5 D6
Chapel Street........................15 B1
Chapel Terrace 33 A1
Chapel Wood 10 G2
Chard Avenue 11 B2
Chard Court 11 B2
Chargot Road 15 B2
Charles Place 29 D5
Charles Street 18 G4
Charlotte Place 30 H1
Charlotte Square 2 H6
Charlotte Street....................20 F6
Charnwood Court 9 D4
Charter Avenue 23 A5
Charteris Close 26 G5
Charteris Crescent 14 G3
Charteris Road 14 G3
Chartley Close 6 G6
Chartwell Court 22 E2
Chatsworth Drive 3 D3
Chatterton Square 20 G3
Chaucer Close (Llanedeyrn) .5 C5
Chaucer Close (Penarth) 26 E1
Chaucer Road 23 B5
Cheam Place 3 B4
Cheddar Crescent 11 B2
Chepstow Close 14 G5
Cheriton Drive 3 B2
Cherry Close (Fairwater) 7 A6
Cherry Close (Murch)...........25 C2
Cherry Close (Penarth) 26 G4
Cherry Orchard Road..............3 A1
Cherry Tree Close 3 D2
Cherrydale Road 14 H3
Cherrydown Close 3 C2/C3
Chervil Close 7 C6
Cherwell Close 7 C6
Cherwell Road 26 F3
Cheshire Close 9 C1
Chester Close 12 E1
Chester Place 16 F5
Chester Street 16 F5
Chesterfield Street 23 D6
Chesterton Road 5 B6
Chestnut Close 25 B3
Chestnut Road 14 G1
Chestnut Tree Close 22 H4
Chestnut Way 26 E2
Cheviot Close 3 A6
Chichester Road 20 G6
Chichester Way 14 H3
Chilcote Street 30 H1
Chiltern Close 3 A6
Chiltern Drive 3 A6
Christina Street.....................16 H5
Chulmleigh Close 11 A3
Church Avenue 20 H6
Church Close 4 E2
Church Cottages 19 B4
Church Hill Close 34 H6
Church Lane (Llanrumney) ...5 D6

Church Lane (Llantwit Major)
....35 C6
Church Meadows 35 C2
Church Place North 20 H6
Church Place South 20 H6
Church Rise 33 B3
Church Road (Barry) 23 D6-24 E1
Church Road (Caerau) 14 F6
Church Road (Canton) 15 D3
Church Road (Cowbridge) ...34 H6
Church Road (Lisvane) 4 E2
Church Road (Llanedeyrn) 5 A5
Church Road (Penarth).........26 G1
Church Road (Pentyrch) 22 E1-F6
Church Road (Rhoose)
....................................27 D4-28 E4
Church Road (Rumney) 11 A4
Church Road (Whitchurch)....8 E3
Church Street (Centre) 18 F5
Church Street (Cowbridge) ..34 F4
Church Street (Llantwit Major)
....35 C6
Church Terrace (Cadoxton) 24 E6
Church Terrace (Roath) 17 B1
Church View 34 G6
Church View Close 20 E4
Churchfields 23 D5
Churchill Close 3 C1
Churchill Terrace 31 A1
Churchill Way 18 H4
Cilfedw 1 A6
Cilgerran Crescent 2 H5
Circle Way East 10 H3
Circle Way West 10 G1
City Hall Road 16 G3
City Road 16 H1-17 A2
Clarbeston Road 8 E5
Clare Drive 34 G3
Clare Gardens 16 F4
Clare Place 16 F4
Clare Road 16 F5
Clare Street 16 F4
Claremont Avenue 11 B3
Claremont Crescent 11 B3
Clarence Embankment 20 H1
Clarence Place 20 H1
Clarence Road 20 H1
Clarendon 10 F1
Clarendon Road 10 F4
Clarewen Drive 10 E2
Clarke Street 14 H3
Clas Canol 8 G4
Clas Cornel 8 G3
Clas Dyfrig 8 G4
Clas Gabriel 8 G4
Clas Heulog 8 G3
Clas Ifor 8 G2
Clas Illtyd 8 H3
Clas Isan 8 H3
Clas Odyn 8 G2
Clas Teilo 8 G4
Clas Ty Wern..........................8 H1
Clas Tyn y Cae 8 G1
Clas Tynewydd 8 F3
Clas Yorath 8 G2
Claude Place 17 A1
Claude Road (Barry) 29 D2-30 E2
Claude Road (Roath) 17 A1
Claude Road West 29 D2
Claymore Place.....................20 G3
Claypool Way 35 C1
Clearwater Way 9 D2
Clearway Court 8 F3
Cleddau Close 6 G6
Cledwyn Close 29 C1
Clement Place 29 D5
Cleve Drive 3 B6
Clevedon Avenue 32 F3
Clevedon Court 11 C1
Clevedon Road......................11 B1
Cliff Court 21 A1
Cliff Hill 26 G3
Cliff Parade 26 G3

Cliff Place 15 B3
Cliff Road 26 G3
Cliff Street 20 H6
Cliff Wood View 29 B4
Cliffside 26 G4
Clifton Street (Barry) 29 D4
Clifton Street (Roath)...........17 B2
Clinton Road 26 F2
Clipper Road 17 C6
Clive Court 15 C3
Clive Crescent 26 H1
Clive Lane 20 F6
Clive Mews 15 C3
Clive Place (Barry Island) ...30 G4
Clive Place (Penarth) 26 G1
Clive Place (Roath) 17 A2
Clive Road (Barry Island) 30 F5
Clive Road (Roath) 15 C2
Clive Street 16 F6-20 F1
Clive Street Lane 16 F6
Clodien Avenue 9 B4
Clos Bryn Melyn 7 A1
Clos Brynderi 2 G6
Clos Caewal 1 B4
Clos Cas Bach 12 F1
Clos Cefn Bychan 22 E1
Clos Cefni 29 C1
Clos Coed y Dafarn 4 E3
Clos Cromwell 2 H4
Clos Dyfnaint 12 F1
Clos Fach 2 H5
Clos Glanaber 12 F1
Clos Glas Llwch 12 F2
Clos Gwern y Mor 12 F1
Clos Gwlad yr Haf 12 F1
Clos Hafodyrynys 12 E1
Clos Hafren 12 F1
Clos Hendre 2 H5
Clos Mabon 2 G5
Clos Maerun 12 F1
Clos Maes yr Mor 12 F1
Clos Manmoel 12 F1
Clos Menter 8 H5
Clos Newydd 8 E3
Clos Pantycosyn 12 F1
Clos Pen y Clawdd 12 E1
Clos Rhiannon 3 A3
Clos Taf 8 E5
Clos Tawe 29 D1
Clos Ton Mawr 2 H4
Clos Tregare 12 F1
Clos Treoda 8 F2
Clos Tyclyd 7 D3
Clos Tyla Bach 6 G6
Clos William 2 G4
Clos y Berllan 12 F1
Clos y Betws 12 F1
Clos y Blaidd 3 A1
Clos y Broch 3 A2
Clos y Bryn 2 F4
Clos y Carlwm 3 A1
Clos y Ceinach 3 A2
Clos y Culfor 12 F1
Clos y Cwarra 13 C4
Clos y Draenog 3 A2
Clos y Dyfrgi 2 H2
Clos y Gof 13 C4
Clos y Gornant 12 F1
Clos y Graig 2 F4
Clos y Gwadd 3 A2
Clos y Nant 14 G1
Clos y Onnen 12 F1
Clos y Rhiw...........................14 E6
Clos y Wenallt 2 F4
Clos y Wern 2 H5
Clos y Wiwer 3 A2
Clos yr Aer 2 H5
Clos yr Ardd 2 G6
Clos yr Hafod 2 H5
Clos yr Onen 35 D4
Close, The 3 C5
Clovelly Crescent 11 A2
Clover Close 7 B6

Clun Terrace...........................9 D5
Clydach Street 16 G6
Clyde Street 17 B3
Clydesmuir Road 17 D2
Clyro Place 8 E4
Coal Pit Lane 6 G1
Coaster Place 17 D6
Coates Place 5 C6
Coates Road 26 E4
Cobol Road 6 G5
Coburn Street 16 H1
Coed Arhyd 13 C5
Coed Arian 8 G4
Coed Bach.............................33 C6
Coed Cochwyn Avenue..........3 A4
Coed Edeyrn 10 F3
Coed Glas Road 2 H5/3 A5
Coed Mawr 33 C6
Coed y Dafarn 4 E3
Coed y Gores 10 G2
Coed y Llyn (Cyncoed) 9 D3
Coed y Llyn (Radyr) 22 H4
Coed y Capel 33 C6
Coed yr Ynn 2 H5
Coedcae Street 16 G6
Coeden Dal 4 G5
Coedriglan Drive 13 C5
Cog Road 32 E1
Cogan Court 20 F5
Cogan Hall Cottages 25 D3
Cogan Hill 20 F5
Cogan Pill Road 20 E4
Cogan Spur Road 20 F5
Cogan Terrace 16 G2
Coigne Terrace 30 H2
Coity Close 6 F6
Colborne Walk......................15 D4
Colchester Avenue 10 F5-H6
Colchester Court...................10 H5
Colcot Road 23 A5-30 E1
Cold Knap Way 29 D5
Coldbrook Road East............24 E6
Coldbrook Road West...........24 E6
Coldstream Terrace 16 F4
Coleford Drive 12 E1
Coleridge Avenue 26 E1
Coleridge Crescent...............23 A5
Coleridge Road 19 D2
Colhugh Close 35 C5
Colhugh Park 35 C6
Colhugh Street 35 C5
Colin Way 14 H3
Collard Crescent...................23 B6
College Close 8 E4
College Field Close 30 E1
College Place 30 E2
College Road (Barry) 30 E2/F2
College Road (Centre) 16 G2
College Road (Llandaff North)
....8 F4
College Street........................35 C6
Collingdon Road 17 A6/21 A1
Colum Drive 16 F1
Colum Place 16 F1
Colum Road 16 F1
Colum Terrace 16 G2
Columbus Close 23 C4
Columbus Walk 16 H5/18 H6
Column Street 31 C1
Colwill Road 8 F4
Colwinstone Close 8 F4
Colwinstone Street 8 E4
Colwyn Road 11 B3
Comeston Street 9 B6
Comet Street 17 A3
Comfrey Close 6 G5
Commercial Road 30 H1
Commercial Street................35 B5
Compass Road 21 C1
Compton Street 16 F5
Connaught Road 17 A1
Constellation Street..............17 B3
Constitution Hill 34 G5

Conway Close 25 C1
Conway Drive 29 C1
Conway Road................15 D2
Conybeare Road (Canton)..15 C2
Conybeare Road (Sully) 32 F1
Cook Road 23 C4
Coopers Lane 34 F4
Copleston Road..............8 F5
Copper Street 17 B3
Copperfield Drive............3 B3
Coppins, The 3 D2
Cora Street....................30 G2
Corbett Road (Cathays)......16 G2
Corbett Road (Llandough)..19 D5
Corinthian Close 20 E4
Cormorant Close 6 E5
Cornelly Close 8 F4
Cornelly Street 8 F4
Cornerswell Lane 26 E1
Cornerswell Place 26 E1
Cornerswell Road............26 E2
Cornfield Close................2 H4
Cornflower Close.............3 C1
Cornish Close 20 G1
Cornwall Rise 23 B6
Cornwall Road................23 C6
Cornwall Street 16 F6
Cornwood Close.............7 A6
Coronation Road............8 H3
Coronation Street 30 G2
Coronation Terrace 20 H6
Corporation Road......16 F6-20 G1
Corwen Crescent 8 F4
Cory Place....................20 G3
Cory Way 30 G3
Coryton Close...............1 D6
Coryton Crescent 1 D6
Coryton Drive 1 D6
Coryton Rise..................1 D6
Cosheston Road 7 C5
Cosmeston Drive 26 F6
Cosslett Place 20 F4
Cotswold Avenue 3 D2-4 E2
Cotswold Court..............10 E1
Cotswold Rise 30 H1
Cottage Close.................3 C3
Cottage Row..................33 A1
Cottrell Road (Plasnewydd) 17 A1
Cottrell Road (Whitchurch) ..8 G2
Cottrell Square 23 C5
Countess Place 26 E2
Countisbury Avenue...5 C6-11 C1
Court Close (Cowbridge)...34 E1
Court Close (Mynachdy)....8 H4
Court Colman 23 C5
Court Newton 30 H1
Court Road (Barry).......30 G2/H1
Court Road (Grangetown)..16 F5
Court Road (Whitchurch) ..8 G4
Courtenay Road (Cadoxton)31 A1
Courtenay Road (Splott)...17 C3
Courtis Road...................14 E4
Courtlands 29 D4
Coveny Street 17 C3
Cowbridge By Pass......34 F5-G2
Cowbridge Road East
.................15 A3-16 F3
Cowbridge Road West ..14 E6-H3
Cowbridge Street............24 E6
Cowper Close.................26 E1
Cowper Court 17 A2
Cowper Place 17 A2
Cowslip Drive.................20 E6
Coychurch Rise..............23 D5
Craddock Street 16 E4
Cradoc Road..................8 H3
Cragside Close...............12 F1
Craig Castell 7 A1
Craig yr Allt...................2 G4
Craig yr Haul Drive..........6 H2
Craiglee Drive................17 A5
Craigmuir Road..............17 D2
Cranbrook Street............16 H2

Cranleigh Rise................11 A3
Cranmer Court...............15 B1
Cranwell Close...............7 D5
Craven Walk 26 G5
Crawley Close 3 A2
Crawshay Court..............35 B4
Crawshay Drive..............35 B4
Crawshay Lane...............16 G5
Crawshay Street.............16 G5
Crediton Road................11 C1
Crescent Close...............34 H3
Crescent, The (Barry)......29 C1
Crescent, The (Fairwater)...14 G2
Cresswell Close..............6 F5
Cresswell Court..............23 C5
Cressy Road...................10 E6
Criccieth Court...............25 C1
Criccieth Place...............11 B3
Crichton Place................18 G6
Crichton Street...............18 G6
Crickhowell Close............14 H4
Crickhowell Road......6 E6-12 E1
Crockherbertown Lane......18 G4
Croescadarn Close 4 H4
Croescadarn Road...........4 H3
Croffta...........................25 A3
Croft Gardens.................32 E2
Croft Street (Cowbridge)...34 G4
Croft Street (Roath).........17 A2
Croft Terrace..................34 G3
Croft y Genau Road..13 D2/22 F6
Crofta.............................3 D4
Cromwell Road...............8 H3
Cross Common Road....25 A3-C4
Cross Hill 29 C5
Cross Place....................9 A6
Cross Street (Barry).........30 G2
Cross Street (Tongwynlais)...1 B4
Crossfield Road...............29 D2
Crossways Road..............14 F4
Crossways Street............30 G1
Crown Way 9 B6
Croyde Avenue...............11 B1
Crumlin Drive 6 F6
Crundale Crescent 3 B5
Crwys Lane 23 D5
Crwys Place...................14 H5
Crwys Road.......9 C6-16 H1
Crystal Avenue................9 C1
Crystal Glen........3 C6-9 C1
Crystal Rise....................9 C1
Crystal Wood Road 9 B1
Culver Close...................26 E4
Cumberland Street 15 D4
Cumnock Place..............17 B4
Cumnock Terrace............17 B4
Cumrae Street................17 B4
Cunningham Close...........9 C2
Cunningham Court 17 A5
Curlew Close..................8 F1
Curlew Crescent 35 C1
Curll Avenue 9 B4
Curran Embankment........16 G6
Curran Road 16 G5
Custom House Place 20 H5
Custom House Street 18 G6
Cwm Barry Way..............29 C3
Cwm Cidy Cottages 29 B3
Cwm Cidy Lane 29 B3
Cwm Gwynlais.................1 C5
Cwm Nofydd....................2 F5
Cwm Parc.....................29 D1
Cwmcarn Close 6 F6
Cwmdare Street...............9 C6
Cwrt Cefn.......................3 D3
Cwrt Deri 2 G5
Cwrt Glas.......................3 B5
Cwrt Heledd...................9 D6
Cwrt Ty Mynydd..............7 A1
Cwrt y Vil Road 26 F2
Cwrt y Vil Road Lower......26 F2
Cwrt yr Ala Lane 14 F6
Cwrt yr Ala Road 14 E6

Cyfarthfa Street 17 A2
Cymmer Street................16 G6
Cymric Close..................14 G3
Cynan Close...................23 D5
Cyncoed Avenue.............10 E1
Cyncoed Crescent...........10 F1
Cyncoed Place 10 E1
Cyncoed Rise 10 E1
Cyncoed Road........4 E5-10 F5
Cyntwell Avenue.............14 E6
Cyntwell Crescent 14 E5
Cyntwell Place 14 E5
Cypress Drive........6 F5-12 G1
Cypress Place 7 C5
Cyril Crescent 17 B2
Cyril Street.....................30 H2

D
Dafydd Place..................23 C5
Daisy Street....................15 C2
Dalcross Street...............9 D6
Dale Avenue...................8 H2
Dale Court 23 C5
Dalmuir Road 17 D2
Dalton Street 9 C6
Dan y Banc Cottages 1 A4
Dan y Bryn.....................22 H4
Dan y Bryn Close 7 A1
Dan y Coed 9 D1
Dan y Coed Rise 10 E1
Dan y Coed Road......3 D6-10 E1
Dan y Graig 1 D5
Dan yr Heol....................9 D1
Danescourt Way..............7 C4
Daniel Close...................32 E2
Daniel Hopkin Close.........35 D5
Daniel Street (Barry).........23 D6
Daniel Street (Cathays)......9 C6
Darby Road.....................17 D5
Darran Street 9 C6
Darren Close...................34 F6
Darren Hill 34 F6
David Davies Road...30 H3/31 A2
David Street (Cadoxton)....24 E5
David Street (Centre)........18 H5
Davies Place...................15 A2
Davies Street..................30 H1
David Street....................9 D6
Davis Street...................17 A4
Davis's Terrace................8 F2
Dawan Close 29 D1
De Braose Close 7 C4
De Burgh Place 16 F4
De Burgh Street...............16 F4
De Clare Court 35 B3
De Croche Place 16 E4
Deans Close...................15 B1
Deans Court 8 F6
Deemuir Road.................17 D1
Deepdale Close...............10 E4
Deepdene Close..............13 C4
Deepfield Close 13 C4
Deepwood Close 13 C4
Deere Close....................14 E5
Deere Place....................14 E5
Deere Road....................14 E5
Deganwy Close 3 A4
Dell, The 5 C5
Delta Street....................15 D4
Den Roche Place.............18 H4
Denbigh Court (Penarth)....26 F2
Denbigh Court (Whitchurch)..8 F1
Denbigh Drive.................35 B3
Denbigh Road 25 C1
Denbigh Street.................15 D1
Denbigh Way 23 B6
Denison Way 13 C4
Denton Road 15 D4
Denys Close...................25 B1
Deri Close......................10 G6
Deri Road 10 F6
Derwen Court 34 F6
Derwen Road 4 E5
Derwent Close.................3 A3

Despenser Gardens 16 F4
Despenser Place 16 F4
Despenser Road 32 E1
Despenser Street............16 F4
Dessmuir Road 17 D2
Devon Avenue 30 G1
Devon Place...................16 F6
Devon Street..................16 F6
Dew Crescent 14 G5
Dewi Court 8 F6
Diamond Street 17 B3
Diana Place....................10 E6
Diana Street 9 D6
Dickens Avenue 5 B6
Digby Close....................7 C5
Digby Street...................30 H2
Dimlands Road................35 C6
Dinas Place....................16 F6
Dinas Road.....................26 E3
Dinas Street...................15 F5
Dingle Close...................29 C4
Dingle Lane....................26 F1
Dingle Road 26 F1
Dingle, The.....................26 G1
Ditchling Court................26 F2
Dobbins Road.................24 F5
Dochdwy Road................20 E4
Dock Road (Barry Island) ...30 G4
Dock Road (Penarth) 20 H6
Dock Street.....................20 F6
Dock View Road 30 F3-H2
Dogfield Street.................9 C6
Dogo Street....................16 E2
Dolgoch Close 11 D2
Dolwen Road 8 F5
Dombey Close.................3 B3
Dominions Arcade............18 G4
Dominions Way 17 C1
Donald Street 9 D6
Donniford Close...............32 F1
Donnington Road 31 C1
Dorchester Avenue 10 F5
Dorchester Mansions 8 E1
Dorothy Avenue...............23 B4
Dorothy Close..................23 B5
Dorset Avenue 30 G1
Dorset Street..................16 F6
Douglas Close.................7 D5
Dovedale Close................10 E4
Dovedale Street..............30 H1
Dovey Close (Barry).........29 C1
Dovey Close (Trowbridge) ..11 D2
Dowlais Road 17 B5
Dowland Road.................26 E4
Downfield Close...............20 E4
Downlands Way 11 A5
Downs Court 23 D4
Downs View.....................34 E1
Downs View Close 34 E1
Downton Rise 11 B5
Downton Road 11 B5
Downtown Grange 11 C5
Doyle Avenue..................14 H1
Doyle Court 14 H1
Drake Walk 17 A5
Drangway 35 C5
Drawlings Close 5 D5
Drive, The (Fairwater) 14 G2
Drive, The (Murch)...........25 C2
Drope Road 13 B4
Dros y Mor.....................26 G3
Dros y Morfa 11 B5
Druids Green 34 H3
Druidstone Road.......6 E4-F1
Drury Close.....................3 B3
Drybrook Close................12 F1
Dryburgh Avenue.............8 H2
Dryden Close...................20 E6
Dryden Road 20 F6
Dryden Terrace 23 B5
Drylla...........................25 A3
Drysgol Road 7 A2
Dudley Court...................21 A2

Dudley Place...................29 D3
Duffryn Avenue 9 D1
Duffryn Close..................9 C1
Duffryn House 25 B2
Duffryn Road 10 E1
Dugdale Walk 16 E4
Duke Street....................18 F4
Dukes Arcade 18 F4
Dulverton Avenue............5 C6
Dulverton Drive 32 F2
Dulwich Gardens............15 C2
Dumballs Road 16 H6-20 H1
Dumfries Place................16 H3
Dummer Close.................6 E6
Duncan Close..................11 D1
Dunkery Close 11 B1
Dunlin Court...................30 G2
Dunraven Close 25 C2
Dunraven House..............16 G4
Dunraven Road...............16 E5
Dunraven Street..............29 C3
Dunsmuir Road 17 D2
Dunster Drive..................32 E2
Dunster Road 5 C6
Durham Street 16 F6
Durleigh Close.................5 B6
Durlston Close 5 A6
Durrell Street 35 B5
Duxford Close..................7 C5
Dyfan Road 23 C6
Dyfrig Close....................16 F6
Dyfrig Court 35 B4
Dyfrig Road....................15 A3
Dyfrig Street (Barry Island) .30 G4
Dyfrig Street (Riverside)....16 E2
Dylan Close....................20 E5
Dylan Crescent 23 D5
Dylan Place 17 A2
Dynevor Road 10 F4
Dyserth Road..................26 F2

E
Eagle Lane 34 F4
Eagle Road.....................35 B1
Eagleswell Road..............35 B3
Earl Crescent 30 G5
Earl Lane........................20 G1
Earl Road.......................20 G1
Earl Street......................20 G1
Earle Place....................15 D4
Earls Court Place.............10 F6
Earls Court Road.............10 F5
Earlswood Court..............9 D4
Earlswood Road 3 B6
East Bay Close.................17 A4
East Canal Wharf.....16 H5/18 G6
East Grove......................17 A2
East Grove Lane 17 A2
East Moors Road 17 A4
East Rise.......................3 C4
East Road.......................31 D1
East Street (Barry)...........30 E3
East Street (Llantwit Major).35 C5
East Tyndall Street...........17 B4
East Wall........................21 A2
Eastbourne Court 24 E5
Eastbrook Close...............25 B1
Eastern Avenue.......5 A6-H5
Eastern Close..................5 D5
Eastgate.........................34 G4
Ebwy Court....................14 G5
Eckley Road....................32 E2
Eclipse Street 17 A3
Eddystone Close..............16 E6
Edgehill Avenue...............2 H4
Edgehill Court..................2 H4
Edinburgh Court..............16 E4
Edington Avenue.............9 D5
Edith Road.....................25 A2
Edmonds Court...............9 D5

Edmund Place 31 B1
Edward Clarke Close 7 D5
Edward House 16 F4
Edward Nicholl Court..........10 F5
Edward Street (Barry) 23 D5
Edward Street (Centre) 18 H4
Egerton Street 15 C3
Egham Street 15 C2
Eglwys Brewis Road 35 C2
Egremont Road 9 D4-10 E5
Eider Close........................6 E5
Eifion Close 23 D5
Elaine Close 3 A3
Elan Close 29 D1
Elan Road...........................3 C6
Elder Wood Close 10 G4
Elderberry Road 7 A6
Eldon Court.......................16 E4
Eleanor Place 20 A2
Eleven Street......................31 C1
Elfed Avenue 25 D1-26 E2
Elfed Green 7 D6
Elfed Way 23 D5
Elford Road.......................14 F4
Elgar Crescent 5 D6
Elgar Road 26 F4
Elizabeth Avenue 23 B4
Elizabeth Flats 16 F5
Elizabethan Court 20 F5
Ellen Street.......................17 A4
Ellesmere Court 11 D1
Ellwood Close...................12 F1
Elm Close 32 F2
Elm Grove.........................24 E5
Elm Grove Lane 25 A2
Elm Grove Place 25 A2
Elm Grove Road 25 A2
Elm House (Hollybush Est.)..7 D1
Elm Street.........................17 A2
Elmfield Close...................11 E1
Elmgrove Road 7 D3
Elmwood Court 17 A2
Elworthy Close..................32 F2
Ely Road 15 A2-B1
Emerald Street 17 B2
Empire House....................21 A1
Emsworth Court................10 F1
Enfield Drive.....................33 C6
Ennerdale Close..................9 D5
Epsom Close 14 H4
Epstein Close......................7 C5
Erskine Court.....................17 C2
Erw Las.............................8 F3
Erw Wen............................2 G5
Erwr Delyn Close 25 D1
Eskdale Close 9 D4
Esplanade 26 H2
Essich Street 10 E6
Ethel Street 15 B3
Eton Court 9 B1
Eton Place 15 D4
Eton Street 29 C3
Eugene Close 6 G5
Eurgan Close 35 C5
Eurwg Crescent...................5 D5
Evans Street......................30 F2
Evansfield Road..................8 E4
Evelyn Street (Barry).........30 G2
Evelyn Street (Butetown) ...20 H1
Evenlode Avenue 26 F3
Everard Street 30 H1
Everard Way.......................9 D3
Everest Avenue 3 B4
Everest Walk 3 C4
Everswell Avenue 14 G2
Everswell Road 14 G2
Ewbank Close....................24 F5
Ewenny Close 23 C5
Ewenny Road......................3 C6
Excalibur Drive 2 H3-3 B2
Excelsior Road....................8 H5
Exeter Mansions.................8 E1
Exford Crescent.................11 A2

Eyre Street 17 C3
F
Faber Way.........................16 E6
Factory Road.....................34 H6
Fair Meadow.....................22 E1
Fairacre Close 3 A2
Fairbrook Close 2 F5
Fairfax Road.........................8 H1
Fairfield Avenue 15 B2
Fairfield Close (Canton) 15 A2
Fairfield Close (Llantwit Major)
....35 B4
Fairfield Crescent 35 B4
Fairfield Rise.....................35 B4
Fairfield Road....................20 G6
Fairfield Street..................23 D6
Fairhaven Close 5 F5
Fairlawns Court...................8 F6
Fairleigh Road...................15 D1
Fairoak Court......................9 D5
Fairoak Mews.....................9 D5
Fairoak Road 9 C6/D5
Fairoaks............................25 B2
Fairthorn Close 3 B2
Fairview Close 5 F5
Fairview Court.....................4 F6
Fairwater Avenue 14 H2
Fairwater Green 14 G2
Fairwater Grove East 15 A1
Fairwater Grove West 15 A1
Fairway, The........................4 F4
Fairways Crescent.............14 F2
Fairwood Close 7 D6
Fairwood Road 7 D6
Falcon Grove.....................26 F6
Falcon Road......................24 F6
Falconwood Drive 13 C4
Falfield Close......................3 C3
Fanny Street..........9 D6/16 G1
Farm Drive...........................9 D3
Farmhouse Way 14 E6
Farmleigh.........................11 B3
Farmville Road..................17 C3
Farthings, The 4 H4
Felbridge Close.................17 A6
Felin Fach 8 F4
Felin Wen............................2 G6
Fen Violet Close................12 G1
Fennel Close (Penarth) 20 E6
Fennel Close (Trowbridge)..6 G5
Fern Drive.........................30 E1
Fern Place 14 G1
Fern Street 15 C2
Ferndale Street 16 F6
Ferntree Drive 5 D6
Ferny Court.......................10 F5
Ferrier Avenue......7 C6/14 G1
Ferry Lane 20 H6
Ferry Road (Butetown).......20 H2
Ferry Road (Grangetown)
..............................20 F2/G4
Festiniog Road.....................8 F5
Fford Celyn........................8 G3
Ffordd Elin 24 F6
Ffordd Las 22 H4
Ffordd Pengam 18 E1/F2
Ffordd y Barcer 13 C4
Ffordd y Brenin ...16 G3/18 F4
Fidlas Avenue......................3 C6
Fidlas Road 3 C5-9 C1
Field View Road................23 D6
Fielding Close......................5 B6
Fields Court.......................16 D2
Fields Park Road...............15 D1
Finchley Road...................14 H2
Firs Avenue.......................14 E1
Firwood Close.....................8 E3
Ffishguard Close 8 F3
Ffishguard Road..................3 B5
Ffishponds Road...............11 B1

Fitzalan Court 17 A3
Fitzalan Place 17 A3
Fitzalan Road....................17 A3
Fitzhamon Avenue 35 C5
Fitzhamon Embankment 16 F4
Fitzhamon Lane.................16 F4
Fitzroy Street 16 H1
Flanders Meadow..............35 C5
Flanders Road...................35 C6
Flax Court 20 E6
Flaxland Avenue..................9 A4
Fleet Way 20 E1
Flint Avenue......................35 B3
Flint Street 9 A6
Flora Street 16 G1
Florence Avenue 23 B4
Florence Street..................17 C2
Florentia Street....................9 C6
Fonmon Crescent 14 G4
Fonmon Park Road 27 B3
Fonmon Road 27 B1-B5
Font y Gary Road 27 B5-D4
Fonthill Place 16 E6
Fontigary Road..................11 C4
Fordwell............................8 F6
Foreland Road....................8 F2
Foreshore Road.................17 D6
Forest Cottages...................1 C3
Forest Court 15 D2
Forest Farm Road 7 B1-D1
Forest Oak Close 4 E4
Forest View.......................14 F2
Forge Place 14 E5
Forrest Road (Canton) 15 B3
Forrest Road (Penarth) 26 F4
Forrest Street.....................20 G1
Forsythia Drive....................4 F4
Fort Street 17 C1
Fortran Road 6 G5
Foster Drive.......................10 G5
Foster Street......................31 A1
Fountain Lane......................6 G5
Four Acre 35 B4
Four Elms Court................17 A2
Four Elms Road.................17 A2
Fouracres Close.................24 F6
Fox Russell Close................4 F5
Fox Street..........................17 C2
Foxglove Close..................14 E4
Foxglove Rise....................20 E6
Francis Road.....................23 C4
Frank Road 14 F3
Franklen Road......................8 H3
Franklen Street..................16 F6
Frederick Street 18 G4
Fremington Place 11 C2
Freshmoor Road................17 C4
Frewer Avenue 14 G2
Friars Road 30 F5/G5
Friary, The..........................18 G4
Frigate Road......................21 B1
Fryatt Street 30 G2
Fulmar Close (Penarth) 20 E6
Fulmar Close (Trowbridge)..6 E5
Furnace Street...................31 C1
Furness Close 14 E5
G
Gabalfa Avenue.......8 E5-G5
Gabalfa Road 8 E5
Gadlys Road East 30 E2
Gadlys Road West 30 D2
Gaen Street.......................29 D3
Gaerwen Close 3 A5
Gainsborough Court 23 A6
Gainsborough Road 20 F6
Galahad Close 4 E4
Gallamuir Road 17 D2
Galston Place....................17 B3
Galston Street....................17 B3
Gardenia Close...................4 F6
Garesfield Street 16 F6
Gareth Close 2 H3
Garrick Drive 3 B3

Garth Close 1 A5
Garth House.......................23 C5
Garth Place..........................8 H4
Garth Street.......................17 A4
Gaskell Close 35 C2
Gaspard Place 29 D5
Gelli Deg 2 G4
Gelligaer Gardens 9 B6
Gelligaer Lane 9 C6
Gelligaer Street...................9 B6
Gelynis Terrace 1 A5
Gelynis Terrace North 1 A5
George Street (Barry) 30 G2
George Street (Butetown) ...21 A1
Georges Row 25 C1
Georgian Close 35 B4
Georgian Way 3 C5
Geraint Close.......................3 A3
Geraint Place.....................23 C6
Geraints Close 34 G6
Geraints Way.....................34 F6
Gernant 2 G6
Gerrard Court 16 E4
Gibbets Hill 34 F5
Gibbonsdown Close 23 C5
Gibbonsdown Rise 23 C5
Gibson Close.......................9 B1
Gilbert Lane East....23 D4-24 E4
Gilbert Lane West 24 E3
Gilbert Place........................8 H4
Gilbert Street 23 D6
Gileston Road 15 D2
Gilian Road 8 E6
Gilwern Crescent 3 B4
Gilwern Place 3 A4
Glades, The 26 H1
Gladstone Court 30 F2
Gladstone Road 30 F2-H1
Gladys Street.......................9 C6
Glamorgan Close 35 B3
Glamorgan Mews 15 D3
Glamorgan Street (Barry)...29 D3
Glamorgan Street (Canton).15 D3
Glan Ely Close...................14 F2
Glan y Mor.........................29 C5
Glan y Mor Road 11 D2
Glan y Nant Road................8 F2
Glan y Nant Terrace............8 F2
Glandovey Grove 11 D1
Glandwr Place 8 F2
Glanmor Crescent 30 E2
Glanmuir Road...................17 D1
Glanrhyd...............................2 G6
Glas Efail............................2 H6
Glas Lyn Close...................29 C1
Glas y Pant 2 E6
Glastonbury Road 32 E1
Glastonbury Terrace...........11 B1
Glebe Place..........................3 C5
Glebe Street (Barry) 23 D6
Glebe Street (Penarth) 20 H6
Glen Affric Close................30 E1
Glen Hafren.......................29 C5
Glen Mavis Way 29 D1
Glen View 9 C1
Glenbrook Drive 24 F5
Glencoe Street 30 G1
Glendale Avenue 3 B4
Gleneagles........................15 A2
Glenmount Way 2 G2
Glenrise Close......................6 G5
Glenroy Street....................16 H1
Glenside Court 10 E5
Glenwood.........................10 F1
Glossop Road....................17 A3
Glossop Terrace.................17 A3
Gloucester Close 23 C6
Gloucester Street 17 B3
Glyn Coed Road ...4 G5-10 G1
Glyn Collen 4 H6
Glyn Eiddew 4 H5
Glyn Rhosyn 4 F5
Glyn Simon Close 7 D4

Glynbridge Close...............23 B4
Glyndwr 26 E2
Glyndwr Road (Barry) 30 E2
Glyndwr Road (Ely) 14 E3
Glynne Street 15 D3
Glynrhondda Street............16 H2
Glynstell Close...................20 E1
Godfrey Street...................17 A4
Goodwin Close 7 C3
Gold Street 17 B2
Goldcrest Drive 4 F6
Goldsland Place 29 D2
Goldsmith Close..................5 B6
Golgate Street...................18 F5
Goodwick Close 23 B5
Goodwick Road.................11 C4
Goodwood Close...............13 C4
Gordon Road.....................16 H2
Gorse Place 14 F1
Gorsedd Gardens Road......16 G3
Goscombe Drive................20 F6
Gough Road 14 F4
Gower Court 29 D2
Gower Street 9 C6
Gradon Close 31 A1
Grafton Close 10 F4
Grafton Terrace 8 H1
Graham Walk 16 E4
Graig Hir 1 A6
Graig Llwyd..........................1 A6
Graig Llwyn Road................4 E1
Graig Road...........................3 D1
Graig View...........................3 D2
Graigwen 1 A5
Grand Avenue 13 D5-14 G3
Grange Avenue 33 B3
Grange Close......................33 B2
Grange Gardens (Grangetown)
....20 G1
Grange Gardens (Llantwit Major)
....35 B4
Grange Place 20 G1
Grange, The 15 A1
Grangetown Link Road
..........................19 D1-20 F3
Grangetown Spur Road......20 F3
Grantham Close 7 D5
Grants Close........................1 B5
Granville Avenue 15 B2
Grasmere Avenue 9 D4
Grassmere Close...............20 E4
Gray Street........................15 D3
Graylands, The 8 G1
Grays Walk 34 F3
Great West Lane.................18 G6
Great Western Court 15 D4
Greave Close 33 B2
Greek Church Street..........16 H5
Green Close 13 D5
Green Farm Lane...............13 D5
Green Farm Road 13 D5
Green Lane (Cadoxton) 24 E5
Green Lane (Murch)...........25 A5
Green Lawns 23 C6
Green Street 16 F4
Green, The (Leckwith).......19 B2
Green, The (Llandaff)..........8 F6
Green, The (Radyr) 7 B2
Greenbanks Drive 29 D1
Greenbay Road..................18 E2
Greencourt Close..................8 G3
Greencroft Avenue 15 A3
Greendale Place 1 C5
Greenfield Avenue (Birchgrove)
....8 H2
Greenfield Avenue (Canton)15 D2
Greenfield Avenue (Dinas Powys)
....25 A1
Greenfield Road..................8 H2
Greenfield Way 34 H5
Greenhaven Rise 20 E5
Greenland Crescent 14 F1
Greenlawns 10 F5

Greenmeadow Close 25 B3
Greenmeadow Drive 1 C4
Greenmeadows 12 E2
Greenock Road 11 D1
Greenside 34 G3
Greenway Avenue 11 C4
Greenway Close 19 D4
Greenway Court 24 F5
Greenway Road 5 D6-11 C4
Greenwich Road 15 B2
Greenwood Lane 13 D2
Greenwood Road 8 E6
Greenwood Street 30 F2
Grenville Road 10 F6
Gresford Close 11 D1
Greyfriars Road 16 G3/18 G4
Greys Drive 35 B3
Griffin Close 33 C5
Grimson Close 32 F2
Grisedale Close 10 E5
Groes Lon 2 G5
Gron Ffordd.......................2 G4
Grosvenor Street 15 C3
Grouse Street 17 A2
Grove Place (Birchgrove)......8 H2
Grove Place (Penarth).......26 F1
Grove Place Lane 26 F1
Grove Terrace 26 F1
Grove Way 11 B4
Grove, The (Barry) 29 D4
Grove, The (Rumney) 11 B4
Groveland Road 8 H2
Grundale Crescent 3 B5
Guenever Close 2 H3
Guest Road 17 C5
Guildford Place 18 H5
Guildford Street 18 H4
Guildhall Place 18 F5
Guthrie Street 30 H1
Guys Road 30 H1
Gwaun Close (Thornhill) 2 H3
Gwaun Close (Whitchurch)...7 D2
Gwendoline Place 17 B3
Gwendoline Street............17 B3
Gwenfo Drive 33 B2
Gwenllian Street 31 B1
Gwennyth Street 9 D6
Gwenog Court 29 D1
Gwent Road 14 E5
Gwernhuddi Road 4 E5
Gwert Close 12 E2
Gwilym Place 23 C5
Gwyn James Court 20 F6
Gwynant Crescent 9 D2
H
Habershon Street.............17 C3
Hackerford Road 4 E5
Hadfield Road.........15 C6-20 E1
Hadley House 26 E4
Hafod Street 16 G5
Hafren Court 15 D2
Hafren Road 30 E2
Haig Place 13 D6
Hailey Court 8 E3
Halsbury Road 15 C2
Halton Close 26 G5
Ham Lane East 35 D4
Ham Lane South 25 C5
Hamilton Court 15 C3
Hamilton Street.................16 E3
Hammond Way 10 F6
Hampstead Walk 13 C5
Hampton Court Road.........10 G5
Hampton Crescent East 4 F4
Hampton Crescent West......4 E4
Hampton Road 9 A3
Hanbury Close 7 D2
Handel Close 26 E4
Hannah Street (Atlantic Wharf)
....17 A6
Hannah Street (Barry).......30 G1
Hanover Court (Cadoxton) .24 F6
Hanover Court (Whitchurch) .8 E1

Hanover Street (Barry) 30 F2
Hanover Street (Canton).....15 D4
Hansome Place 16 E6
Harbour Road.........29 D4-30 E5
Harbour View Road 20 G6
Harding Close 35 C2
Hardwicke Court 15 A1
Hardy Close 23 C4
Hardy Place 17 A2
Harford Close 7 D2
Harlech Close 25 C1
Harlech Court......................8 F1
Harlech Drive 25 B1
Harlech Gardens 23 A5
Harlech Road 11 C4
Harlequins Court 17 C1
Harold Street 17 C2
Harpur Street 16 G5
Harriet Street (Cathays) 16 H1
Harriet Street (Penarth) 20 F6
Harrington Court 14 E6
Harris Avenue 11 C3
Harrismith Road 10 E6
Harrison Way 20 G3
Harrowby Lane 20 H1
Harrowby Place 20 H1
Harrowby Street 20 H1
Hartland Road 11 A2
Hartley Place 16 E6
Harvey Place 15 D3
Harvey Street....................31 A1
Hastings Avenue 26 E1
Hastings Close 26 E1
Hathaway Place 24 E5
Hatherleigh Road 11 A4
Haul Fryn 2 E5
Havant Close 27 D5
Havelock Place 16 F6
Havelock Street 18 F5
Havenwood Drive 2 H2
Haverford Way 14 G5
Hawfinch Close 4 F6
Hawkwood Close 7 A6
Hawthorn Avenue 26 E2
Hawthorn Close 25 B2
Hawthorn Road 29 C3
Hawthorn Road East 8 E4
Hawthorn Road West 8 E4
Hawthorns, The 4 G6
Haxby Court 17 A6
Hayes Bridge Road...........18 G5
Hayes Lane 31 B3
Hayes Road 31 B3
Hayes, The 18 G5
Hazel Grove 25 B3
Hazel Place 7 B6
Hazel Road 26 E2
Hazel Tree Close 22 H4
Hazeldene Avenue 9 C5
Hazeldene Close 23 C6
Hazelhurst Court 8 E3
Hazelhurst Flats 8 E4
Hazelhurst Road 8 E3
Hazelwood Drive 6 E6
Hazlitt Close 5 B5
Heath Avenue 20 E6
Heath Halt Road.................9 C2
Heath Mead 9 C2
Heath Park Avenue 9 C2
Heath Park Court 9 C3
Heath Park Crescent 9 C3
Heath Park Drive 9 C2
Heath Park Lane 9 C3
Heath Street 16 F4
Heath Way 9 A1
Heathbrook 3 C6
Heathcliffe Close 5 D5
Heather Avenue 15 A3
Heather Way 14 G1
Heathers, The 30 E2
Heathfield Drive 23 A6
Heathfield Place 9 A5
Heathfield Road 9 A5

Heathwood Court 9 B2
Heathwood Grove 9 C3
Heathwood Road.........9 A3-D1
Heddfan North 4 H6
Heddfan South 4 H6
Hedel Road........................15 B3
Helen Place 17 B2
Helen Street......................17 B2
Hellas Drive 33 D5
Hendre Close 15 B1
Hendre Gardens...............15 B1
Hendre Road 11 D1-12 E2
Hendy Street 9 D6
Hengoed Close 14 F5
Henllys Road 4 E6
Henry Street (Butetown)....17 A6
Henry Street (Cadoxton) ...31 B1
Heol Aer 2 H5
Heol Aradur 7 C4
Heol Blakemore 8 E2
Heol Booker 7 D2
Heol Briwnant 2 G4
Heol Brynglas 2 F5
Heol Cae Rhys 2 H6
Heol Carnau 14 G6
Heol Carne 8 G3
Heol Cattwg 8 G4
Heol Cefn On 3 C2
Heol Chappell 8 E2
Heol Coed Cae 8 G3
Heol Dennant 14 G1
Heol Derlwyn 2 G5
Heol Deva 14 F6
Heol Dewi Sant..................30 E2
Heol Dolwen 8 H3
Heol Don 8 E3
Heol Dyfed 9 A2
Heol Ebwy 14 G5
Heol Eglwys 14 G5
Heol Erwin 2 H4
Heol Esgyn 9 D1
Heol Fair 8 F6
Heol Ffynnon Wen...............2 E5
Heol Gabriel 8 G4
Heol Ger y Felin 35 B4
Heol Goch 22 E1
Heol Gwent 9 A2
Heol Gwilym 7 C6
Heol Gwrgan 8 G2
Heol Gwyndaf 3 C6
Heol Gwynedd 9 A2
Heol Harlech 15 A1
Heol Hendre 2 H5
Heol Hir 3 B3
Heol Iestyn 8 G2
Heol Ifor 8 G2
Heol Isaf (Radyr)........1 A6-7 B3
Heol Isaf (Rhiwbina)...........2 G4
Heol Iscoed 2 H5
Heol Lewis 2 G4
Heol Liangan 8 G1
Heol Llanishen Fach ..2 G5-H4
Heol Mabon 2 G5
Heol Madoc 8 G3
Heol Maes Eirwg 12 F1
Heol Mathew 8 E2
Heol Merioneth 35 B2
Heol Merlin 3B6
Heol Muston 14 G2
Heol Nant Castan 2 H5
Heol Nest 8 G2
Heol Pantycelyn (Barry) 30 E2
Heol Pantycelyn (Canton) ...2 E6
Heol Pantyderi 2 E6
Heol Pantyrhyn 2 E6
Heol Pencarreg 8 F5
Heol Penlan........................7 D2
Heol Pennar 14 G5
Heol Pentre Felin 35 A4
Heol Pentwyn 2 E6
Heol Penyfai........................8 G3
Heol Peredur 3 A3
Heol Powys 9 A1

Heol Poyston 14 F6
Heol Pwllyplaca 12 F1
Heol Rhayader 7 D3
Heol Seddon........................7 C5
Heol Sirwhi 29 C1
Heol Solva 14 G5
Heol St. Denys 3 C2
Heol Stradling 8 G2
Heol Syr Lewis.....................1 A5
Heol Trefgarne 14 F6
Heol Trelai 14 E6/H5
Heol Trenewydd 14 F6
Heol Trostre 12 F1
Heol Tyn y Cae 8 G1
Heol Tyn y Coed 2 H5
Heol Uchaf 2 F4
Heol Urban 8 G3
Heol Wen 2 F6
Heol Wernlas 8 H3
Heol y Berllan 14 F5
Heol y Bont 2 G6
Heol y Bryn (Barry)...........29 C5
Heol y Bryn (Rhiwbina) 2 F6
Heol y Cadno 3 A2
Heol y Carw 3 A2
Heol y Castell 14 F6
Heol y Cawl 25 A2
Heol y Coed (Llantwit Major)
....35 D4
Heol y Coed (Rhiwbina) 2 F5
Heol y Delyn 3 D3-4 E2
Heol y Deri 2 F5
Heol y Felin (Ely)..............14 H3
Heol y Felin (Llantwit Major)35 D5
Heol y Felin (Rhiwbina)........2 G5
Heol y Fforest 1 C3-D1
Heol y Forlan 8 F1
Heol y Frenhines 25 A3
Heol y Gaer (Barry) 29 C5
Heol y Gaer (Caerau) 14 F5
Heol y Gors 8 G3
Heol y Nant (Barry)...........23 D6
Heol y Nant (Birchgrove) 8 G1
Heol y Parc 5 A1
Heol y Pavin 8 F6
Heol y Pentre 22 E2
Heol y Rhosog 11 C6
Heol y Waun 8 G4
Heol y Wern 2 H5
Heol yr Efail 2 A6
Heol yr Odyn.....................14 E6
Heol yr Ynys 1 A3
Herbert March Close 7 C4
Herbert Street (Barry) 23 C6
Herbert Street (Centre)
.................................16 H5/18 H6
Herbert Street (Gabalfa).......9 A6
Herbert Terrace.................26 G1
Hereford Street 16 F6
Heritage Park 6 F5
Hermon Hill 1 B4
Heron Road 11 C4
Hewell Court 20 F1
Hewell Street 20 F6
Hickman Road 26 G1
Hickory Court 17 B4
High Meadow 35 C5
High Street (Barry) 30 E3
High Street (Centre)..........18 F4
High Street (Cowbridge)....34 F4
High Street (Llandaff)..........8 F6
High Street (Llantwit Major).35 B5
High Street (Penarth) 20 G6
High Street Arcade 18 F4
High View Road 20 G6
Highbridge Close 32 G2
Highbury Place 14 E4
Highbury Road 14 F4
Highcroft Walk 11 B2
Highfield Close 25 C1
Highfield Road (Barry).......23 A5
Highfield Road (Heath).........9 C3
Highfields 8 E5

Highlands...........................11 A5
Highlight Lane.............33 C5/D5
Highmead Road 14 F4
Highwalls Avenue.............24 H1
Highwalls End...................25 A1
Highwalls Road 25 A1
Hilary Close 3 B4
Hilda Street 30 E3
Hiles Road 14 F4
Hill Snook Road 14 F4
Hill Street (Barry)..............30 H1
Hill Street (Penarth)..........20 H6
Hill Terrace 20 G6
Hill View 14 F1
Hillary Rise 30 H1-31 A1
Hillcot Close 3 C3
Hillcrest Close.....................3 B2
Hillrise 10 E2
Hills Street 18 G5
Hillside Close 24 E6
Hillside Court 10 E5
Hillside Drive 34 G3
Hillside Villas 24 E6
Hilton Place 8 E3
Hinchcliffe Avenue 23 A5
Hinton Street 17 C4
Hirst Crescent....................7 C6
Hirwain Street...................16 G1
Hodge Hall 16 H2
Hodges Row 16 H6
Hodges Square 16 H6
Holden Road 19 D1
Holgate Close.....................7 C4
Holland Way 23 D5
Holly Cottages....................8 G3
Holly Grove 3 C1
Holly Road 10 G4
Holly Terrace 8 F5
Hollybush Estate 7 D1
Hollybush Heights...............4 F6
Hollybush Rise 10 F1
Hollybush Road 10 F1
Hollycroft Close 14 H3
Hollyrood Close 33 C5
Holmes Street...................31 A1
Holmesdale Court.............20 F2
Holmesdale Street 20 G1
Holms Court......................32 E2
Holmsdale Place 26 G2
Holmside 12 E2
Holmview Court 11 C2
Holmwood Close 10 E3
Holton Road 30 F3-31 A1
Holy Court 29 D4
Homelands Road 8 H1
Homeside House...............26 H1
Honeysuckle Close............14 F1
Honiton Road 5 C6
Hood Road 30 E3-G3
Hope Court 16 H1
Hope Street 18 G6
Hope Terrace 17 B3
Hopyard Meadow 34 F5
Hornbeam Close 6 G6
Hornchurch Close 7 D2
Horton Way 31 C1
Horwood Close 17 C2
Houlston Court 17 D2
Housman Close...................5 B5
Howard Court....................29 D2
Howard Gardens 17 A3
Howard Place....................17 A3
Howard Street 17 A3
Howard Terrace.................17 A3
Howardian Close...............10 G6
Howell Road 4 E5
Howells Crescent..............15 C1
Hughes Close 7 D4
Hunt Close 3 B4
Hunter Street (Butetown) ...20 H1
Hunter Street (Cadoxton) ...31 A1
Hunters Ridge 10 E3
Hurford Place......................4 E5

Hurman Street.....20 H1	Kelvin Road.....9 D6	Laburnum Way (Murch).....25 B3	Lily Street.....17 A2	Lon y Ffin.....13 D4
Huron Crescent.....9 D3	Kemeys Road.....27 D4	Laburnum Way (Penarth)...26 E2	Lime Close.....7 B3	Lon y Groes.....9 A3
Hurston Street.....15 D4	Kemys Road.....8 H4	Lady Margaret Court.....10 G6	Lime Grove.....7 A6	Lon y Mynydd.....2 H6
Hydrangea Close.....4 F6	Kendrick Road.....30 F2	Lady Margaret Terrace.....17 B3	Limebourne Court.....8 F4	Lon y Nant.....2 H6
Hywel Crescent.....23 C6	Kenfig Road.....9 A4	Lady Mary Road.....9 D4	Limes Court.....34 G4	Lon y Parc.....8 G2
I	Kenilworth Court.....15 A2	Ladysmith Road.....10 F6	Limes, The.....34 G4	Lon y Rhydd.....2 G5
Iestyn Street.....15 D2	Kenilworth House.....16 G4	Lake Hill Drive.....34 G4	Limeslade Close.....15 A2	Lon y Winci.....2 F5
Iestynian Avenue.....15 D2	Kenilworth Road.....23 D6	Lake Road East.....9 D2-D4	Limewood Close.....6 E6	Lon y Ysgubor.....2 F5
Ilchester Road.....11 C1	Kenley Close.....7 D6	Lake Road North.....9 C2	Lincoln Court.....10 F2	Lon yr Efail.....14 E6
Ilex Close.....3 B5	Kenmuir Road.....17 D2	Lake Road West.....9 D2-D4	Lincoln Street.....15 C3	Long Meadow Drive.....23 C6
Ilfracombe Crescent.....11 C2	Kennedy Rise.....29 D2	Lake View Close.....9 D3	Linden Avenue.....10 E5	Longacre Close.....24 F5
Illtyd Avenue.....35 C5	Kennerleigh Road.....11 A3	Lake View Court.....9 D3	Linden Grove.....11 B3	Longcross Court.....17A2
Illtyd Road.....14 E3	Kenneth Treasure Court.....5 D6	Lakeside.....29 C5	Lingholm Close.....12 F1	Longcross Street.....17 A3
Ilminster Close.....23 D6	Kennington Close.....3 A3	Lakeside Drive.....9 D2	Linnet Close.....4 F6	Longhouse Close.....3 D3
Ilminster Street.....23 D6	Kensington Avenue.....15 B2	Lakin Drive.....33 C5	Linway Court.....15 C5	Longleat Close.....3 D3
Ilton Road.....10 F6	Kenson Close.....27 B5	Laleston Close (Barry).....23 C5	Lionel Road.....15 C3	Longmeadow Court.....34 F4
Inchmarnock Street.....17 B4	Kenson Hill.....27 B1	Laleston Close (Caerau).....14 F5	Liscum Way.....33 D5	Longmeadow Drive.....25 B3
Inglefield Avenue.....9 B5	Kent Green.....30 F1	Lamberton Street.....17 B4	Lisnagarvey Court.....2 E5	Longreach Close.....13 C4
Insole Close.....15 A1	Kent Street.....20 G1	Lambourne Crescent.....3 B6	Lisvane House.....19 D3	Longships Road.....21 B3
Insole Court.....15 A1	Kenwood Road.....14 E4	Lamby Way.....11 A1-C4	Lisvane Road.....3 C4-4 E3	Longspears Avenue.....9 A4
Insole Gardens.....15 A1	Kenyon Road.....18 E1	Landaff Chase.....8 E6	Lisvane Street.....9 B6	Longwood Drive.....1 B6-7 B1
Insole Grove East.....15 A1	Keppoch Street.....16 H1	Landaff Place.....15 C2	Little Brynhill Lane.....33 D5	Lonsdale Road.....10 G4
Insole Grove West.....15 A1	Kerrigan Close.....7 C6	Landaff Square.....5 D6	Little Dock Street.....20 F6	Lord Street.....20 H6
Insole Place.....15 A2	Kerrycroy Street.....17 B3	Lanes, The.....35 C5	Little Mill.....8 F4	Lothian Crescent.....10 F4
Instow Place.....11 C1	Kestrel Close.....4 F6	Langdale Close.....10 E5	Little Moors Hill.....24 E6	Loudoun Square.....16 H6
Inverness Place.....9 D6	Kestrel Drive.....20 G3	Langham Way.....16 E6	Little Orchard.....25 C2	Louisa Place.....21 A1
Iolo Place.....23 D5	Kestrel Way.....26 G5	Langland Road.....11 C4	Littlecroft Avenue.....15 A3	Love Lane (Centre).....18 H5
Ipswich Road.....10 G6	Keswick Avenue.....9 D4	Langlands Road.....24 F5	Littleton Street.....16 E4	Love Lane (Cowbridge)...34 G5
Iron Street.....17 B3	Ketteringham Close.....32 E1	Langport Avenue.....11 C1	Llanbedr Road.....14 H2	Loveluck Court.....35 C5
Ironbridge Road.....1 B5	Kewstoke Avenue.....11 B2	Lanhydrock Close.....12 F1	Llanbleddian Gardens.....16 H2	Lowdon Terrace.....30 F3
Irving Place.....30 F2	Kewstoke Close.....11 B2	Lansdowne Avenue.....8 H1	Llanbradach Street.....16 G6	Lower Acre.....14 E6
Islamic Court.....16 H5	Kewstoke Place.....11 B2	Lansdowne Avenue East...15 C4	Llancaiach Road.....8 G3	Lower Cathedral Road.....16 F3
Island Road.....30 E3	Keyes Avenue.....9 C2	Lansdowne Avenue West.15 B3	Llandaff Close.....26 F3	Lower Holmes Street.....31 A1
Island View Road.....32 G3	Keynsham Road.....8 H2	Lansdowne Road.....15 B3	Llandaff Road.....15 D2	Lower Morel Street.....30 H2
Islwyn Way.....23 D5	Keyston Road.....7 C5	Lapwing Close.....26 F5	Llandefgedd Close.....3 B2	Lower Pyke Road.....30 H2
Ivor Jones Court.....10 F1	Kilcattan Street.....17 B3	Larch Court.....1 C4	Llandeilo Close.....25 C2	Lowfield Drive.....3 A2
Ivor Street.....30 F5	Kilgetty Close.....14 F5	Larch Grove.....3 D2	Llandennis Avenue....9 D1-10 E1	Lowther Court.....16 H2
Ivy Street (Canton).....15 C2	Kilgetty Court.....14 E1	Larch House (Hollybush Est.)7 D1	Llandennis Green.....10 E1	Lowther Road.....16 H2
Ivy Street (Penarth).....26 F1	Kimberley Road.....10 E6	Larchwood.....33 B3	Llandennis Road.....9 C1	Lucas Close.....24 F5
Ivydale.....3 C2	Kimberley Terrace.....3 B5	Larkwood Avenue.....26 F3	Llandetty Road.....14 G2	Lucas Street.....9 D6
J	Kincraig Street.....16 H1	Laugharne Avenue.....11 C4	Llandinam Crescent.....8 G6	Lucknow Street.....16 F6
Jackrow Square.....14 F5	King George V Drive East.....9 C4	Laugharne Court.....23 C5	Llandinam Road.....30 E2	Ludlow Close.....8 G2
Jackson Road.....14 E4	King George V Drive North..9 B2	Laugharne Road.....11 C4	Llandogo Road.....6 E6	Ludlow Lane.....26 G1
Jade Close.....3 D1	King George V Drive West...9 B3	Launcelot Crescent.....3 A3	Llandough Hill.....20 E4	Ludlow Street (Grangetown)
James Street (Butetown).....21 A1	King George VII Avenue.....16 G2	Laura Street.....24 F6	Llandough Street.....16 G2	.....20 G1
James Street (Cadoxton).....31 B1	King Street.....20 H6	Laureate Close.....5 B6	Llandovery Close.....14 F5	Ludlow Street (Penarth)...20 G6
Janet Street.....17 B3	King Wood Close.....10 G4	Laurel Cottages.....13 D2	Llandow Road.....14 G4	Lundy Close.....3 B5
Jasmine Drive.....6 F6	Kingarth Street.....17 B4	Laurel Court (Barry).....29 D4	Llandudno Road.....11 C3	Lydford Close.....8 G1
Jasper Close.....7 D5	Kingfisher Close.....6 E6	Laurel Court (Fairwater).....14 G1	Llandyfrig Close.....25 C2	Lydstep Crescent.....8 G5
Jellicoe Court.....17 A5	Kingfisher Square.....35 C1	Lauriston Close.....14 F6	Llanedeyrn Close.....16 F6	Lydstep Flats.....8 G5
Jellicoe Gardens.....9 C2	Kings Avenue.....7 B2	Lauriston Park.....14 F6	Llanedeyrn Drive...10 G1-G4	Lydstep Road.....23 B5
Jenkin Street.....23 D6	Kings Ride.....24 H2	Lavender Grove.....7 B6/14 F1	Llanedeyrn Home.....10 G3	Lynch Blosse Close.....7 D5
Jenner Road.....29 D2-30 E2	Kings Road (Pontcanna).....16 E2	Lavernock Road (Penarth)	Llanedeyrn Road.....10 F4	Lyncroft Close.....5 D5
Jenner Street.....31 A1	Kings Road (Radyr).....7 B2	.....26 E2-F6	Llaneirwg Way.....5 D6-6 E1	Lyndhurst Street.....16 E4
Jestyn Close (Dinas Powys)25 B1	Kingscombe Cottages.....34 H6	Lavernock Road (Sully).....32 G2	Llanfair Road.....15 D2	Lynmouth Crescent.....11 A4
Jestyn Close (Michaelston-s-Ely)	Kingsland Crescent.....30 G2	Lawrenny Avenue.....15 C5	Llangattock Road.....14 H2	Lynmouth Drive.....32 E2
.....13 C5	Kingsland Road (Canton)...15 B3	Laytonia Avenue.....9 A4	Llanmaes Road.....35 B5	Lynton Close (Llanrumney).11 A3
Jevan Close.....7 C4	Kingsland Road (Whitchurch)7 D3	Le Pouliguen Way.....35 B5	Llanmihangel Road.....34 H5	Lynton Close (Sully).....32 F1
Jewel Street.....30 H2	Kingsley Close.....32 F2	Lead Street.....17 B3	Llanover Street.....23 D6	Lynton Place.....11 A3
Jim Driscoll Way.....20 G1	Kingston Road.....16 E4	Leamington Road.....8 G1	Llanquian Close.....34 G4	Lynton Terrace.....11 A3
John Morgan Close.....7 D4	Kingsway.....18 F4	Leckwith Avenue.....15 D4	Llanquian Road.....34 E1	Lynwood Court.....17 A2
John Street (Cadoxton).....31 B1	Kingway Road.....17 A6	Leckwith Close.....15 D5	Llantwit Major By Pass..35 A4-C1	Lyon Close.....20 E2
John Street (Centre).....18 H6	Kingwood Court.....9 D4	Leckwith House.....23 C5	Llantwit Major Road (Cowbridge)	Lyric Way.....3 B3
John Street (Penarth).....20 H6	Kipling Close (Llanrumney)...5 B6	Leckwith Place.....15 D4	.....34 G6	M
Johns Lane.....8 F5	Kipling Close (Penarth).....20 F6	Lee Close (Dinas Powys)...25 B1	Llantwit Major Road (Llantwit	Maberley Court.....3 C6
Johnston Road.....2 H4	Kirby Court.....17 A5	Lee Close (Llanedeyrn)...10 F3	Major).....35 A6	Macauley Avenue.....5 B6
Jones Court.....18 F5	Kirkland Court.....10 E6	Lee Court.....11 C2	Llantwit Road.....35 C1	Macdonald Close.....13 D5
Jonquil Close.....6 F6	Kirkwall Court.....17 D2	Lee Road.....30 H1	Llantwit Street.....30 G2	Macdonald Place.....14 E5
Joseph Parry Close.....20 E5	Kirton Close.....7 D6	Leigh Close.....35 C3	Llewellyn Avenue.....14 E3	Macdonald Road.....13 D5
Jubilee Lane.....20 H6	Kitchener Close.....15 D4	Lennox Green.....31 B1	Llewellyn Street.....30 H1	Machen Close.....8 H3
Jubilee Street.....16 F5	Knap Car Terrace.....29 B5	Leoline Close.....34 F5	Lloyd Avenue.....30 E1	Machen Place.....16 F4
Junction Lock Road.....21 A1	Knightswell Close.....13 D6	Letton Road.....17 A5	Llwynpia Cottages.....1 A6	Machen Street (Grangetown)
Junction Terrace.....7 B2	Knightswell Road.....13 D6	Lettons Way, The.....25 A1	Llys Hafn.....1 A2	.....16 F6
Justin Close.....10 E3	Knowberry Avenue.....26 G5	Letty Street.....16 G1	Locks Road.....21 A3	Machen Street (Penarth)...26 F1
K	Knox Road.....17 A3	Leven Close.....9 D2	Loddon Close.....7 D2	Mackintosh Place.....9 D6
Kames Place.....17 A3	Kyle Avenue.....8 G2	Lewis Road (East Moors)...17 C4	Lon Cefn Mably.....27 C4	Madoc Close.....25 C2
Kane Close.....3 B6	Kyle Crescent.....8 G2	Lewis Road (Llandough)...19 D4	Lon Fach.....2 G6	Madoc Road.....17 D2
Kathleen Street.....29 D3	Kymin Road.....26 H1	Lewis Street (Barry).....29 D3	Lon Ucha.....2 G6	Maelfa.....10 G3
Keats Way.....23 B5	Kymin Terrace.....26 H1	Lewis Street (Canton).....16 E4	Lon od Nant.....35 D4	Maelog Place.....9 A5
Keen Road.....17 B4	Kyveilog Street.....16 E2	Library Street.....15 D3	Lon y Dderwen.....2 G6	Maelog Road.....8 H3
Kelston Close.....8 E2	L	Lidmore Road.....29 C2	Lon y Castell.....14 F6	Maendy Road.....34 G2
Kelston Place.....8 E2	Laburnum Close.....23 C6	Lilac Close.....7 B6	Lon y Dail.....2 G6	Maerdy Lane.....4 E3
Kelston Road.....8 E2	Laburnum Place.....14 G1		Lon y Deri.....2 G6	Maes Glas.....8 F3

Maes Lloi 34 E2
Maes y Bryn.........................1 A6
Maes y Coed (Barry) 29 C5
Maes y Coed (Birchgrove) 9 A1
Maes y Coed (Rhiwbina) 2 F6
Maes y Crochan......................6 G6
Maes y Cwm Street 30 G1
Maes y Deri 2 G6
Maes y Felin.........................8 G1
Maes y Llech Cottages.........7 A4
Maes y Parc 8 G1
Maes y Parc Road................5 A1
Maes yr Awel 7 A1
Maes yr Haf 2 E5
Mafeking Road 10 F6
Magellan Close 23 C5
Magnolia Close 4 F6
Magpie Road 35 C1
Maillards Haven 26 G4
Main Avenue 10 G6
Main Road 1 A3
Main Street 23 D6-24 E6
Maindy Road 9 B6/16 G1
Maitland Court 16 F5
Maitland Place 16 F5
Maitland Street 9 A5
Major Road 15 D4
Maldwyn Street 15 D2
Malefant Street 9 C6
Mallard Close 5 D6
Mallard Way 26 F5
Malmesmead Road................5 C6
Malpas Close 6 F6
Maltings, The 4 H4
Malvern Drive 3 A6
Mandeville Place 16 E4
Mandeville Street.................16 E4
Manitoba Close 10 E2
Manobier Close 25 C1
Manod Road 8 F5
Manor Close...........................8 G2
Manor Court...........................8 F1
Manor Park 35 D4
Manor Rise 8 G3
Manor Street 9 B5
Manor Way 8 G2
Manorbier Court 23 C5
Manorbier Crescent 11 B3
Mansell Avenue 13 C5
Mansfield Street 16 E4
Manston Close 7 D5
Maple Close 23 C6
Maple Road (Fairwater) 7 A6
Maple Road (Penarth) 26 E2
Maple Tree Close 22 H4
Maplewood Avenue................8 E4
Maplewood Court 8 E4
Maplewood Flats 8 E4
Marchwood Close 11 C2
Marcross Road 13 D5
Mardy Road 11 C5-12 G5
Mardy Street 16 F5
Margam Road 9 A5
Margaret Avenue 23 B4
Maria Court..........................16 H5
Maria Street.........................16 H5
Marine Drive 29 B5
Marine Parade 26 G3
Mariners Heights 20 H6
Marion Court..........................3 D4
Marion Street 17 C3
Marionville Gardens 14 H1
Mark Street 16 F4
Market Place 15 D3
Market Road 15 D3
Market Street (Barry) 16 G1
Market Street (Cathays) 16 G1
Market Street (Tongwynlais) .1 B4
Marl Court 20 F2
Marlborough Close 24 E6
Marlborough House 16 G4
Marlborough Road...10 E6-17 B1
Marlborough Terrace............16 F1
Marloes Close 23 B6

Marloes Road 14 E3
Marquis Close 30 G5
Marshall Close 7 D5
Marsham Court.......................7 B2
Marshfield Road 6 H2
Martin Road 17 D5
Mary Ann Street 18 H5
Mary Street 8 E5
Maryport Road 9 D4
Masefield Road 26 E1
Mathias Close 10 G5
Matthew Road 27 B4
Matthew Terrace 19 D6
Maughan Lane 20 H6
Maughan Terrace.................20 H6
Maureen Avenue 14 G3
Mavis Grove 8 H1
Maxwell Road 11 B3
May Street 9 C6
Mayfair Drive 3 A2
Mayfield Avenue 15 B3
Mayflower Avenue..................2 H4
Mayhill Close 3 B2
Maynard Court 8 F6
McCale Avenue 14 H1
McQuade Place 30 F5
Meadow Close 4 F5
Meadow Lane 26 F4
Meadow Street 15 D2
Meadow View 24 E5
Meadowbank Court 7 C5
Meadowcroft 28 E4
Meadowlark Close 6 E6
Meadowside 25 D2
Meadowsweet Drive 12 G1
Meadowview Court...............32 E1
Meadwvale Road 11 D1
Meggitt Road 23 A5
Meirion Close 23 D5
Meirion Place.......................17 D2
Meirwen Drive 13 D6
Melbourne Close 34 G4
Melbourne Court 8 G1
Melbourne Lane 3 C5
Melbourne Road 3 C5
Meliden Lane 26 F1
Meliden Road 26 F1
Melingriffith Drive...................7 D2
Melrose Avenue 10 F6
Melrose Close 6 E5
Melrose Court (Canton) 15 D2
Melrose Court (Roath) 10 E5
Melrose Street 23 D6
Melville Avenue 6 E5
Melville Close 23 B4
Menai Way 11 D1
Mendip Road 11 A2
Mendip View 24 E6
Merches Gardens 16 F5
Merches Place 16 F5
Mercia Road 17 D2
Meredith Road 17 D3
Merevale.................................24 H2
Merganser Court 30 G2
Meridian Court 9 A5
Merioneth House 26 F2
Merioneth Place 23 B6
Merlin Close (Llanishen).......3 A3
Merlin Close (Penarth) 26 F5
Merlin Place.........................23 C5
Merthyr Rd. (Tongwynlais)1B4-C5
Merthyr Rd. (Whitchurch).8 F2/H3
Merthyr St. (Barry Island)...30 G2
Merthyr Street (Cathays) 16 G1
Mervinian Close 17 A5
Mervyn Road (Splott) 17 D2
Mervyn Road (Whitchurch) ...8 G2
Meteor Street 17 B3
Methodist Lane....................35 C5
Merthyr Dyfan Road.......23 B6/B4
Meyrick Road 13 D5
Michaelston Court (Ely) 14 F5

Michaelston Court (Michaelston-
  s-Ely) 13 C5
Michaelston Place 23 D4
Michaelston Road 13 C4
Middlegate Court 34 F4
Milburn Close 27 C4
Mile Road 25 D4-26 E5
Mill Close (Dinas Powys) 25 A2
Mill Close (Llanishen)............3 C4
Mill Court 3 C3
Mill Hill Court 14 H3
Mill Lane (Castleton) 6 H1
Mill Lane (Centre) 18 G6
Mill Lane (Landaff)...............15 C1
Mill Lane (Llanrumney).........5 C5
Mill Lay Lane 35 C3
Mill Park 34 G5
Mill Place (Ely) 14 H3
Mill Place (Lisvane) 3 D2
Mill Road (Dinas Powys) 25 A2
Mill Road (Ely) 14 H3
Mill Road (Lisvane) 3 C4
Mill Road (Tongwynlais) 1 B4
Mill Terrace.........................33 A1
Millbrook Close 25 A1
Millbrook Heights 25 A1
Millbrook Park 3 D2
Millbrook Road 25 A1
Millfield 3 C2
Millfield Close 11 D1
Millfield Drive 34 G3
Millgate 3 D4
Millheath Drive 3 C3
Millicent Street.....................18 G5
Millrace Close 3 C3
Millwood 3 C3
Millwood Rise 29 C3
Milton Close 35 C3
Milton Place.........................14 H1
Milton Road (Barry) 23 B5
Milton Road (Penarth) 26 E1
Milton Street 17 A2
Milverton Road 6 H4
Milward Road 30 H1
Min y Coed 1 A6
Min y Mor 3 C5
Min y Nant 2 G6
Minafon 2 G4
Minavon 8 F1
Minehead Avenue 32 E2
Minehead Road 11 C1
Minister Street 16 G1
Minny Street 9 C6
Minsmere Close 6 G6
Minster Close 24 E5
Minster Road 17 C1
Miskin Street (Barry) 29 D4
Miskin Street (Cathays) 16 G1
Mitre Court 8 F6
Mitre Place 8 F6
Mitredale Close 9 D4
Moira Place 17 A3
Moira Street 17 A3
Moira Terrace 17 A3
Mona Place 17 D2
Monkstone Close 26 E5
Monkstone Rise 11 C2
Monmouth House 26 F2
Monmouth Street 16 F5
Monmouth Way 23 B6
Montgomery Road 30 E3
Montgomery Street...............10 E6
Monthermer Road 9 C6
Moor King Close 12 G1
Moorby Court 17 A5
Moordale Road 20 G1
Moore Close 14 F4
Moore Road 14 E4
Moorland Place 17 C3
Moorland Road 17 C2/C4
Moors Lane (Canton) 15 B4
Moors Lane (Ocean Park)...17 B4
Morel Street..........................30 G1

Morfa Cottages....................35 A6
Morfa Crescent....................11 D2
Morfa Lane 33 B3
Morgan Street (Barry) 30 H2
Morgan Street (Centre) 17 A4
Morgans Arcade...................18 G5
Morlais Street (Cadoxton) ...31 A1
Morlais Street (Plasnewydd).9 D5
Morningside Walk.................23 B4
Morris Avenue 2 H4-3 A4
Morris Finer Close................14 H4
Mortimer Road 15 D2
Mostyn Road 13 D43
Mount Pleasant 30 H1
Mount Pleasant Avenue.......11 C1
Mount Pleasant Lane 11 C1
Mount Road 25 A2
Mount Stuart Square 21 A1
Mount, The (Dinas Powys)..25 A2
Mount, The (Lisvane) 3 D1
Mountbatten Close 9 C2
Mountbatten Road................23 C4
Mountjoy Avenue..................26 E1
Mountjoy Close 26 E1
Mountjoy Crescent 26 E1
Mountjoy Lane 26 E1
Mountjoy Place.....................26 E1
Moy Road 16 H1
Muirton Road 17 D2
Mulberry Court 29 D4
Mullins Avenue 11 D2
Mundy Place 16 G1
Munro Place 30 E1
Mur Gwyn 2 G5
Murch Crescent 25 C2
Murch Road..........................25 B1
Murlande Way 28 F4
Murray Walk 16 E4
Murrayfield Road 8 H2
Museum Avenue 16 G2
Museum Place 16 H2
Mylo Griffiths Close 7 C4
Mynachdy Road..........8 H4/9 A5
Myrtle Close.........................26 E2
Myrtle Grove 24 E6
N
Nailsea Court 32 F2
Nant Fawr Close 9 D1
Nant Fawr Crescent 9 D1
Nant Fawr Road 9 D1
Nant Isaf 33 B2
Nant Talwg Way 29 C2
Nant y Adar 35 D4
Nant y Drope 13 C4
Nant y Pepra 13 C5
Nant y Plac 13 C5
Nant y Rhos.........................13 C5
Nant yr Arthur 13 C5
Nant yr Dowlais 13 C5
Nant yr Ely 13 C5
Narberth Court 23 C5
Narberth Road 14 G4
Neale Street.........................30 F1
Neath Street 17 C4
Nelson Court........................17 A4
Nelson Road 23 C4
Nesta Road 15 C3
Nettleford Road 17 D2
Neville Place 16 F4
Neville Street 16 F4
Nevin Crescent 11 C3
New Forest View 34 G3
New House Court 23 A3
New Road 11 A5- C5
New Zealand Road.................9 B5
Newborough Avenue..............3 B5
Newby Court.........................17 A5
Newent Road 12 F1
Newfoundland Road...............9 B5
Newgale Close 23 B5
Newgale Place 14 G4
Newlands Court......................3 C4
Newlands Street 30 F2

Newminster Road.................17 C1
Newport Road 6 H1-17 A3
Newport Road Lane 17 A3
Newport Street 20 G1
Newton Road (Canton) 16 E5
Newton Road (Trowbridge)
  ....12 E4-F5
Newton Street 30 H1
Newtown Court.....................17 A3
Newydd Court..........................1 B5
Neyland Court 23 C5
Neyland Place 14 G5
Nicholl Court........................35 B4
Nicholson Webb Close...........7 C4
Nightingale Place 25 B2
Ninian Park Road 16 E4
Ninian Road.............9 D5-10 E6
Nora Street 9 C6
Norbury Avenue 14 H2
Norbury Court.......................14 H2
Norbury Road.......................14 H2
Nordale Rise 24 F6
Nordale Road 35 C4
Norfolk Court 7 A1
Norfolk Street 15 C3
Norman Cottages 19 A4
Norman Road 8 G3
Norman Street........................9 D6
Norris Close 20 E6
Norsemen Close 27 C4
North Clive Street 16 F6
North Cottages 25 A1
North Edward Street.............18 H4
North Luton Place.................17 A3
North Morgan Street.............16 E3
North Park Road 17 C2
North Pentwyn Road 5 B2-B5
North Rise 3 D4
North Road (Cadoxton)........24 G6
North Road (Cowbridge) 34 F4
North Road (Maindy)..9 A4-16 G3
North Street 16 F6
North View 1 A1
North Walk 30 E1
Northam Avenue 11 A2
Northcliffe............................21 A6
Northcliffe Drive...................20 H6
Northcote Lane 16 H2
Northcote Street 16 H2
Northcote Terrace 31 A1
Northern Avenue 2 E6-8 H3
Northlands 11 A5
Northumberland Street.........15 C4
Norton Avenue 9 A3
Norwich Road.......................10 H6
Norwood 3 B3
Norwood Court 17 B2
Norwood Crescent...............24 F6
Nottage Road 14 F4
Nottingham Street 15 C3
Nurseries, The.....................27 D4
Nursery Cottages 25 A3
Nurston Close 27 B4
O
O'Donnell Road 23 D6
Oak Court (Penarth) 26 E2
Oak Court (Tongwynlais) 1 B3
Oak House (Hollybush Est.)..1 B6
Oak Tree Close 22 H4
Oak Wood Avenue 10 G4
Oakdene Close 10 E3
Oakfield Road 33 D5
Oakfield Street 2 H2
Oakford Close 4 G4
Oaklands 19 B6
Oaklands Close 5 D6
Oakleafe Drive 3 A3
Oakley Place........................20 F1
Oakmead Close 23 B5
Oakmeadow Court................12 E1
Oakmeadow Drive................12 E1
Oakridge (East) 3 B2
Oakridge (West) 3 B3

Oaks, The............3 D3
Oakway............14 F1
Oakwood Close............20 E5
Oban Street............23 D6
Ocean Park............17 B4
Ocean Way............17 B5/C5
Odet Court............1 D6
Odyns Fee............27 B4
Ogmore Place............23 C5
Ogmore Road............14 F5
Ogwen Drive............10 E1
Okehampton Avenue............5 C5
Old Barry Road............20 F5
Old Church Road............8 F2
Old Clipper Road............21 C1
Old Farm Mews............25 A2
Old Hill............5 D6
Old Malt House............25 A2
Old Market............33 B3
Old Mill Road (Cadoxton)...24 E6
Old Mill Road (Lisvane)............3 C3
Old Newport Road............6 E5
Old Port Road............33 B1
Old Vicarage Close............3 C4
Old Village Road............29 D4
Oldwell Court............10 E5
Ollivant Close............7 C4
Ontario Way............10 E2
Orange Grove............7 B6
Orbit Street............17 A2
Orchard Castle............3 A3
Orchard Close (Cowbridge) 34 E1
Orchard Close (Llantwit Major)
............35 C2
Orchard Close (Wenvoe) 33 B2
Orchard Crescent............25 B2
Orchard Drive (Barry)............23 C6
Orchard Drive (Whitchurch)..8 F2
Orchard Grove............1 A5
Orchard Lodge............35 C2
Orchard Park............5 D6
Orchard Place............15 D3
Orchard Rise............26 E1
Orchid Close............12 G1
Ordell Street............17 B3
Oregano Close............6 G5
Orion Court............17 A3
Ormonde Close............10 G4
Osborne Square............16 E6
Osprey Close............6 E5
Osprey Court (Barry)............30 G2
Osprey Court (Penarth)............26 F6
Oswestry Close............11 B4
Othery Place............5 C5
Ovington Terrace............15 C2
Owain Close............10 E3
Owens Close............30 F1
Owens Court............8 H3
Oxford Arcade............18 G5
Oxford Lane............17 A2
Oxford Street (Barry)............29 C4
Oxford Street (Roath)............17 A2
Oxwich Close............14 H2
Oyster Bend............32 F3
P
Pace Close............7 C5
Padarn Close............9 D2
Paddock Place............23 D6
Paddock, The (Cowbridge).34 G3
Paddock, The (Lisvane)............3 C2
Paddock, The (Roath)............10 E5
Paddocks, The (Penarth)....26 G4
Paget Lane............16 F6
Paget Place............20 H6
Paget Road (Barry Island)...30 E5
Paget Road (Penarth)............20 H6
Paget Street............16 F6-20 F1
Paget Terrace............20 H6
Palace Avenue............15 B1
Palace Court............10 E1
Palace Road............15 C1
Palmer Street............24 F5
Palmerston Road............31 B1
Palmerstown Cottages............24 F5

Palmerstown House............24 F5
Pant Bach House............8 H2
Pant Glas............5 A6
Pant Tawel Lane............22 G4
Pantbach Avenue............8 H3
Pantbach House............8 H2
Pantbach Place............8 H3
Pantbach Road............2 G6-8 H3
Panteg Close............13 C5
Panteg Mews............15 C2
Pantglas............22 E2
Pantgwynlais............1 B4
Pantmawr Court............2 E5
Pantmawr Road............2 E5
Pantycelyn Road............20 E5
Pantyderi Close............14 F5
Paper Mill Road............15 B3
Parade, The (Barry)............29 D5
Parade, The (Murch)............25 B2
Parade, The (Plasnewydd)..17 A3
Parade, The (Whitchurch)...8 E3
Parc Hafod............8 E1
Parc y Ty Glas............3 A5
Pardoe Crescent............30 F1
Park Avenue (Barry)............29 D4
Park Avenue (Whitchurch)...8 E1
Park Crescent (Barry)............29 D3
Park Crescent (Whitchurch)..8 E1
Park End Court............9 D1
Park End Lane............9 D1
Park Grove............16 H2
Park Lane (Centre)...16 H3/18 H4
Park Lane (Whitchurch)............8 E1
Park Place............16 G2/18 G4
Park Road (Barry)............29 C4
Park Road (Dinas Powys)...25 A1
Park Road (Penarth)............26 G2
Park Road (Radyr)............7 A1
Park Road (Whitchurch)............8 E1
Park Street............18 F6
Park View............8 E1
Park View Court (Llandough)
............20 E1
Park View Court (Riverside)
............16 F4
Park View Court (Whitchurch)
............8 E1
Parker Place............14 E5
Parker Road............14 E5
Parkfield Place............9 A6
Parkland Walk............29 D3
Parkstone Avenue............6 E5
Parkwell Road............4 H3-5 A2
Parracombe Close............5 B6
Parracombe Crescent............5 B6
Parry Road............29 D4
Parry Street............15 D3
Partridge Lane............17 A2
Partridge Road (Llantwit Major)
............35 B1
Partridge Road (Roath)............17 A2
Pascal Close............6 G5
Pascal Court............17 A2
Pastures, The............23 A6
Patchway Crescent............11 A3
Patterdale Close............9 D5
Pavaland Close............12 F1
Peach Place............14 G1
Pearl Place............17 B3
Pearl Street............17 B3/C2
Pearson Street............17 C3
Pedair Erw Road............9 A2
Pellett Street............18 H5
Pembridge Drive............20 F6
Pembroke Close............25 B2
Pembroke Court............8 F1
Pembroke Place (Barry)............30 E3
Pembroke Place (Llantwit Major)
............35 B3
Pembroke Road............15 C3
Pembroke Terrace............20 H6
Pen y Bryn (Barry)............29 B5
Pen y Bryn (Cadoxton)............24 F6

Pen y Bryn Place............9 A5
Pen y Bryn Road (Cyncoed) .4 E6
Pen y Bryn Road (Gabalfa)...9 B4
Pen y Bryn Way............9 A5
Pen y Cefn............2 H3
Pen y Dre............2 F6
Pen y Groes Avenue............2 H6
Pen y Lan............34 F1
Pen y Lan Court............10 E4
Pen y Lan House............10 F5
Pen y Lan Oval............10 E4
Pen y Lan Place............10 E4
Pen y Lan Road (Llandough)
............20 E4
Pen y Lan Road (Roath) 10 E6-F5
Pen y Lan Terrace............10 F5
Pen y Peel Road............15 D3
Pen y Turnpike Cottages....25 A1
Pen y Turnpike Road
............19 C3-25 A1
Pen y Turnpike View............20 E6
Pen y Wain Lane............9 D6
Pen y Wain Place............10 E6
Pen y Wain Road............9 D6
Pen y Waun............25 B2
Penally Road............14 H4
Penarth Head Lane............21 A6
Penarth Portway............20 G5
Penarth Road............16 G5-20 F5
Penbury Court............1 A5
Pencader Road............14 G3
Pencisely Avenue............15 B2
Pencisely Crescent............15 B2
Pencisely Rise............15 B2
Pencisely Road............15 B2
Pencoedtre Road............23 C3/D5
Pendine Close............23 B5
Pendine Road............14 G3
Pendoylan Close............23 D4
Pendoylan Court............14 H3
Pendragon Close............3 A3
Pendraw Place............9 D1
Pendwallt Road............1 D6
Pendyris Street............16 F5
Penedre............8 F6
Penford Court............17 A2
Pengam Road............17 D1
Pengwern Road............14 G3
Penhevad Street............16 F6
Penhill Close............15 C2
Penhill Court............15 D2
Penhill Road............15 D2
Penlan Rise............20 E5
Penline Court............8 F2
Penline Road............8 F2
Penline Street............17 A2
Penllyn Court............23 C4
Penllyn Road............15 D4
Penmaen Walk............13 C5
Penmark Green............13 D4
Penmark Road............13 D5
Pennant Crescent............10 E1
Pennard Place............9 A4
Pennine Close............3 A6
Pennsylvania............10 F2
Penny Lane............34 F4
Pennyroyal Close............6 G5
Penrhos............22 H3
Penrhos Crescent............11 C3
Penrhyn Close............11 D1
Pensarn Road............12 E2
Pent Lee............4 G6
Pentland Close............3 A6
Pentre Bach Court............6 F5
Pentre Gardens............16 F5/G5
Pentre Place............16 F6
Pentre Street............16 F6
Pentrebane Road............7 A6/13 D1
Pentrebane Street............20 F1
Pentwyn............7 A1-22 H3
Pentwyn Court............2 E6
Pentwyn Drive............4 H5-10 G1
Pentwyn Road............4 F4-5 A6
Pentyrch Street............9 B6

Penydarren Drive............7 D2
Penygarn Road............14 G3
Penygraig............2 G4
Pepys Crescent............11 B1
Percival Close............2 H3
Perclose............25 B2
Percy Smith Road............35 C2
Percy Street............16 G5
Perrots Close............14 H1
Peterswell Road............29 D2
Petherton Place............11 C1
Pethybridge Road............14 E3
Petrel Close............26 G5
Philadelphia Close............24 F6
Philip Street............15 D4
Philippa Freeth Court............30 G2
Phillip Close............8 H1
Philog Court............8 H3
Philog, The............8 H3
Phyllis Street............30 F4
Picadilly............34 H6
Pickwick Close............3 B3
Picton Court............35 B4
Picton Street............16 E3
Picton Walk............16 E4
Piercefield Place............17 B2
Pill Street............20 F6
Pilton Place............9 A5
Pine Court............1 C3
Pine Tree Close............22 H3
Pine Wood Crescent............10 G4
Pinecrest Drive............3 B2
Pinehurst Road............14 F1
Pines, The............8 F2
Pinewood Close............20 E5
Piper Close............7 C5
Pitman Lane............16 E3
Pitman Street............16 E3
Pitmedden Close............12 F1
Planet Street............17 A3
Plantagenet Street............16 F4
Plas Cleddau............29 D1
Plas Essyllt............25 B2
Plas Mawr............7 C6-14 G1
Plas Melin............8 E3
Plas Newydd............8 F3
Plas Pamir............20 H5
Plas St. Andresse............20 H5
Plas St. Pol de Leon............20 H5
Plas Taliesin............20 H5
Plas Treoda............8 G3
Plas y Biswail............12 F1
Plas y Coed............9 D4
Plas y Delyn............4 E2
Plas y Llan............8 F2
Plasnewydd Road............17 A1
Plasnewydd Square............17 A1
Plasnewydd Street............17 A1
Plassey Square............20 G6
Plassey Street............20 G6
Plasturton Avenue............16 E2
Plasturton Gardens............16 E3
Plasturton Place............16 E3
Pleasant View............23 A5
Plover Road............26 G2
Plymouth Cottages............7 B3
Plymouth Drive............7 B2
Plymouth Road. 30 F5
Plymouth Street............18 G4
Plymouth Wood Close............14 G3
Plymouth Wood Crescent..14 F3
Plymouth Wood Road............14 G3
Pomeroy Street............20 H1
Pommergelli Road............7 D3
Pontalun Close............23 C5
Pontcanna Court............15 C1
Pontcanna Place............15 D2
Pontcanna Street............16 E2
Pontfaen............4 F4
Pontrilas Close............13 C6
Pontypridd Road............29 C1
Pontypridd Street............23 D6
Poplar Close............7 B6
Poplar Court............23 C5

Poplar House (Hollybush Est.)
............7 D1
Poplar Road............7 B6-14 G1
Poppyfield Close............6 E6
Porlock Drive............32 E2
Porlock Road............5 C6
Port Madoc Road............12 E2
Port Mews............23 B3
Port Road (Barry)............33 D5
Port Road (Fonmon)......27 A3-C3
Port Road (Merthyr Dyfan)
............23 B3-C3
Port Road (Rhoose)..28 F2-29 A2
Port Road East............23 A5
Port Road West............29 C1-33 D1
Portfield Crescent............3 B6
Porth y Castell............29 B4
Porth y Green Close............34 G5
Porthamal Gardens............8 H1
Porthamal Road............8 G1
Porthcawl Road............14 F5
Porthkerry Place............9 A5
Porthkerry Road (Barry)
............29 D3-30 E3
Porthkerry Road (Rhoose)
............28 E4-F3
Portland Close............26 G3
Portland Place............3 D3
Portmanmoor Road............17 C4
Portmanmoor Road Lane ...17 C4
Pound Field............35 C5
Pound Lane............33 A3
Powderham Drive............16 E5
Powis View............24 E6
Powys Close............25 B1
Powys Drive............25 B1
Powys Gardens............25 B1
Powys Place............25 B1
Powys Road............26 F3
Precinct, The............35 B5
Prendergast Place............14 G6
Prestatyn Road............11 D2
Preswylfa Street............15 C2
Price Avenue............23 D6
Pritchard Close............7 D5
Proctor Close............29 D2
Promenade (Barry Island) ..30 F5
Promenade (Barry)............29 C6
Prospect Drive............15 A1
Providence Place............2 E6
Pum Erw Road............9 A2
Purbeck Street............15 C3
Purcell Road (Llanrumney) ...5 D6
Purcell Road (Penarth)............26 E4
Purdey Close............33 D6
Pwll Mawr Avenue............11 C4
Pwll Mawr Court............11 C4
Pwll Mellin Lane............14 H1
Pwllhelli Court............11 C3
Pwllhelyg............1 C5
Pwllmelin Road............7 C6
Pyke Street............30 G1
Pyle Road............14 F5
Pyra Court............29 D4
Q
Quarella Street............30 H1
Quarry Close............14 F1
Quarry Crescent............14 F1
Quarry Dale............11 B5

Quarry Hill House 17 A4
Quarry Road.......................7 D4
Quay Street.......................18 F5
Queen Anne Square...........16 F1
Queen Gate Tunnel............21 A1
Queen Street (Barry) 29 D3-30 E3
Queen Street (Centre) 18 G4
Queen Street (Tongwynlais) .1 B4
Queens Arcade 18 G4
Queens Road 20 H6
Queens Road South 21 B3
Queens Way 30 G4
Queensberry Road 10 G4
Queenwood........................10 G4
Queenwood Close.............10 E3
Quentin Street 9 A5
R
Rachael Close 7 C4
Radnor Court....................15 C3
Radnor Green...................23 B6
Radnor House 26 F2
Radnor Road (Canton).......15 C3
Radnor Road (Llantwit Major)
....35 B3
Radwen Mews 16 F3
Radyr Court Close...............8 E5
Radyr Court House 7 C4
Radyr Court Rise 7 D5
Radyr Court Road 7 D4-8 E5
Radyr Farm Road................7 B3
Radyr Place 8 H5
Radyr Road 7 B3
Raglan Close (Murch) 25 C2
Raglan Close (St. Mellons)...6 F6
Raglan House 16 G4
Raglande Court 35 D5
Railway Crescent 17 B3
Railway Houses................27 A5
Railway Street (Maindy) 9 A6
Railway Street (Splott)......17 B3
Railway Terrace (Murch)....25 C1
Railway Terrace (Penarth)..26 G1
Railway Terrace (Riverside)16 E4
Railway Terrace (Tongwynlais)
....1 B4
Railway Walk 26 G4
Raisdale Road 26 G3
Raldan Close....................23 D5
Raleigh Walk 17 A5
Rambler Close....................3 B2
Ramsey Road 23 C5
Rannoch Drive 10 E2
Raven Way 26 F6
Ravens Court 10 G5
Ravensbrook 1 A5
Ravenshoe Road...............24 F6
Rawden Place 16 F4
Rectory Close 33 B3
Rectory Court....................26 G1
Rectory Road 30 H1
Rectory Road (Canton)......15 D3
Rectory Road (Penarth).....26 G1
Rectory Road Lane............26 G1
Red House Road 14 F3
Red House Crescent.........14 F3
Red House Place...............14 G3
Red House Road 14 F3
Redberth Close 23 B5
Redbrink Court 14 F3
Redbrink Crescent............30 G5
Redcliffe Avenue...............15 B3
Redlands Avenue..............25 D1
Redlands House................25 D1
Redlands Road 20 E6-26 E2
Redlaver Street.................16 F6
Redwell Court 10 F5
Redwood Close (Llantwit Major)
....35 C3
Redwood Close (St. Mellons)6 E6
Rees Court 35 B4
Regency Close 35 B4
Regent Street....................30 F2
Regina Terrace 15 C2

Reigate Close 3 A2
Relf Road 11 C3
Rennie Street....................16 E4
Restway Court.....................7 C4
Restways 7 C5
Retford Court.......................8 G3
Retreat, The 10 F5
Rheidol Close 3 C5
Rheidol Drive 29 C1
Rhigos Gardens 9 B6
Rhigos Street......................9 B6
Rhiwbina Hill 1 D1-2 F5
Rhiwderyn Close 13 C6
Rhiwlas 2 H3
Rhododendron Close 4 F6
Rhoose Road 28 E4
Rhos Llan 2 G5
Rhosili Avenue..................11 C2
Rhosili Road 11 C3
Rhuddlan Way...................25 C1
Rhydhelig Avenue 9 A3
Rhydypenau Close 9 C1
Rhydypenau Road....4 E6-9 C1
Rhyll Road.........................11 C3
Rhymney River Bridge Road
....10 H6
Rhymney Street 16 H1
Rhymney Terrace..............16 H1
Richard House...................16 F4
Richard Lewis Close 7 D5
Richard Street (Barry).......30 F2
Richard Street (Cathays) ...16 G1
Richards Place 17 B2
Richards Terrace 17 B2
Richmond Court 17 A2
Richmond Crescent 16 H2
Richmond Road.................16 H1
Richs Road..........................8 H3
Ridgeway...........................3 C2
Ridgeway Road (Barry)......33 D5
Ridgeway Road (Llanrumney)
....11 A3
Risca Close 6 F6
Rise, The 3 C4
River View 8 F5/G6
River View Court 8 E5
River Walk (Cowbridge)....34 G5
River Walk (Llantwit Major) .35 B6
Riverdale (Llandaff)...........14 G3
Riversdale (Fairwater)........7 C4
Riverside Place 31 B1
Riverside Terrace 15 A3
Roath Court 17 B1
Roath Court Place.............17 B1
Roath Court Road 17 B1
Roath Dock Road..............17 B6
Robert Street (Barry).........30 H2
Robert Street (Caerau).....15 A3
Robert Street (Cathays) 9 C6
Robin Close 4 F6
Robin Hill 25 B2
Robins Lane 23 D6
Robinswood Close.............26 F3
Robinswood Crescent.......26 F3
Roche Crescent 7 B6
Rochester Mansions...........8 E1
Rockrose Way...................20 E6
Rockwood Road 1 A1
Roden Court 17 A2
Rogersmoor Close.............26 F2
Rogerstone Close 6 F6
Rolls Street........................16 E4
Romilly Avenue 29 D4
Romilly Court.....................29 D4
Romilly Crescent 15 D2
Romilly Park Road 29 C4
Romilly Place.....................15 C3
Romilly Road (Barry)..........29 D3
Romilly Road (Canton).......15 C2
Romilly Road (Rhoose) 28 E4
Romilly Road West............15 C2
Romney Walk 20 F6
Rompney Terrace..............11 B5

Ronald Place.....................14 G3
Rook Close........................35 C1
Rookery Wood...................32 E2
Rookwood Avenue 8 E6
Rookwood Close 8 E6
Rookwood Street...............16 F6
Roper Close 7 C5
Rose Street 17 A2
Roseberry Place 26 F2
Rosedale Close 14 F1
Rosemount Place................9 A4
Rosewood Close 3 D2
Rossett Close 3 D1
Rossetti Close 7 D4
Rothesay House 16 H6
Round Wood 10 G2
Round Wood Close............10 G4
Roundel Close 3 B1
Rover Way 17 D1-21 D1/18 E4
Rowan Close.....................26 G4
Rowan Court (Barry) 29 D4
Rowan Court (Llandaff) 15 B1
Rowan Way 3 D2
Roxborough Garden Court .26 G2
Roxby Court.............16 H5/18 H6
Royal Arcade 18 G5
Royal Close 20 G6
Royal Stuart Lane 20 H1
Royde Close......................13 C5
Ruby Street.........................17 B2
Rudry Road 4 E2
Rudry Street (Grangetown) .16 F6
Rudry Street (Penarth) 26 F1
Runcorn Close (Cadoxton)..24 F6
Runcorn Close (Llanrumney) 5 D5
Runway Road 18 E2
Rushbrook Close.................7 D3
Ruskin Close 5 B6
Russell Street....................16 H2
Ruthen Terrace 30 E2
Ruthin Gardens 16 H2
Rutland Close....................33 C5
Rutland Street....................16 F5
Ryder Street......................16 E3
S
Sable Close 3 D1
Sackville Avenue.................9 B4
Saffron Drive 6 G5
Salisbury Avenue...............26 F2
Salisbury Close..................26 F2
Salisbury Court..................26 F2
Salisbury Road (Barry).......29 D3
Salisbury Road (Cathays)..16 H2
Salop Place 20 H6
Salop Street 20 G6
Salvia Close 6 F6
Sanatorium Road...............15 B4
Sanctuary Court................13 D6
Sanctuary, The..................13 D6
Sanderling Drive..................6 E6
Sandon Place 16 H4/18 H5
Sandon Road 17 A3
Sandon Street........17 A4/18 H5
Sandpiper Close..................6 E5
Sandringham Close 33 D5
Sandringham Road 10 E6
Sandwell Court 20 E5
Sandy Lane 6 H3
Sanquahar Street 17 B4
Sapele Drive 17 B4
Sapphire Street 17 B2
Sarn Court.........................23 C5
Saunders Road 18 G6
Saundersfoot Close 14 G6
School Street 18 H6
Schooner Way 17 A5
Scott Court 9 D4
Scott Road.........................18 F6
Sea View Terrace 24 E6
Seager Cottages 10 H6
Seager Drive 20 G3
Sealawns 29 D6
Seaview Cottages 5 D6

Seaview Court 26 H1
Seaview Place 35 C5
Seaview Terrace 33 A1
Seawall Road 17 D3-18 E3
Second Avenue.................10 G6
Sedgemoor Road................5 C6
Selwyn Morris Court..........17 C4
Sen Place 16 H2
Senghenydd House 16 G2
Senghenydd Road 16 G1
Senni Close.......................29 D1
Sevenoaks Road 14 E4
Sevenoaks Street...............20 G1
Severn Avenue..................29 C1
Severn Court 16 E3
Severn Grove 15 D2
Severn Road......................16 E3
Seymour Street 17 C2
Seys Close.........................34 F5
Seys Court.........................35 B4
Shaftesbury Close...............3 B2
Shakespeare Avenue........26 E1
Shakespeare Court 17 A2
Shakespeare Drive............35 C4
Shakespeare Road 23 B5
Shakespeare Street...........17 A2
Shamrock Road.................14 F1
Sharpe Close 10 G6
Shaw Close 5 B6
Shears Road 15 A2
Shearwater Close (Penarth)26 G6
Sheerwater Close (St. Mellons)
....6 E6
Shelburn Close..................16 E5
Shelley Crescent (Barry) ...23 B5
Shelley Crescent (Penarth) .26 F1
Shelley Walk 17 A2
Shepley Court 7 B4
Sherbourne Avenue............4 E6
Sherbourne Close..............33 C5
Sheridan Close 5 B6
Sherwood Court 7 C6
Shirley Close.....................24 F5
Shirley Road........................9 D5
Silver Birch Close 8 G4
Silver Jubilee Cottages 14 G4
Silver Street......................17 B2
Silverstone Close 5 D5
Sinclair Drive 10 G6
Singleton Road..................17 C4
Sir Ivor Place 25 B2
Skaithmuir Road................17 D2
Skelmuir Road...................17 D2
Skomer Road 23 B5
Slade Close 32 F1
Slade Road 23 B6
Slade Wood House 23 C5
Slocombe Cottages...........15 C2
Sloper Road...........15 D5-16 E6
Smeaton Close..................27 B4
Smeaton Street.................16 E4
Smithies Avenue................32 F2
Sneyd Street......................16 E2
Snipe Street.......................17 A2
Snowden Road..................14 E4
Soberton Avenue 9 B5
Solent Road.......................24 F6
Solva Avenue 3 C5
Solva Close 23 B6
Somerset Court 5 B6
Somerset Road East..........30 F1
Somerset Road West.........30 F1
Somerset Street.................16 F5
Somerset View...................32 F3
Sophia Close.....................16 F3
Sophia Walk......................16 F3
South Clive Street..............20 F2
South Court Road..............10 F5
South Lodge........................6 F2
South Luton Place 17 A3
South Morgan Place...........16 E4
South Park Road 17 C3
South Rise...........................3 D5

South Road.........................32 E2
South View (Rhoose) 27 D5
South View (Ty Rhiw).........1 A1
South View Drive...............11 C2
South Walk........................30 E1
Southbourne Court............30 G5
Southern Way 10 H4
Southesk Place 29 D5
Southey Street (Barry).......30 F2
Southey Street (Roath) 17 A2
Southminster Road............17 B1
Southra 25 A3
Sovereign Chase...............10 E4
Spencer Drive 19 D4
Spencer Street (Barry).......30 F2
Spencer Street (Cathays) ...9 D6
Spencers Row 8 F6
Spinney Close 14 F3
Spinney, The 10 F4
Spires Walk 23 D5
Spitzkop............................35 C5
Splott Road.......................17 C3
Spring Gardens Place 17 C1
Spring Gardens Terrace ...17 C1
Spring Grove 3 C3
Spring Meadow Road 11 C5
Spring Street.......................31 B1
Springfield Close 33 B3
Springfield Gardens............1 A5
Springfield Place 15 D3
Springfield Rise 23 D6
Springhurst Close................1 A6
Springwood.......................10 E2
Spruce Close 17 B4
Square.............................35 C5
Square, The 25 A2
St. Lythans Road 29 D2
St. Agatha Road 9 A3
St. Agnes Court 17 C2
St. Agnes Road 9 A3
St. Aiden Crescent 9 A3
St. Aidens Rise..................24 E6
St. Albans Avenue 9 A3
St. Ambrose Close.............25 A2
St. Ambrose Road...............9 A3
St. Andrews Crescent........16 H3
St. Andrews Lane...............16 H2
St. Andrews Place..............16 H2
St. Andrews Road (Barry) ...30 F1
St. Andrews Road (St. Andrews
Major).................24 F1-H2
St. Andrews Road (Wenvoe)
....23 D1
St. Angela Road 9 A3
St. Annes Avenue..............16 H2
St. Anns Court...................23 C5
St. Anthony Road 9 B3
St. Arvans Crescent 6 E6
St. Asaph Close 9 A1
St. Athan Road 34 H3
St. Augustine Road 9A3
St. Augustines Crescent....21 A6
St. Augustines Place 20 H6
St. Augustines Road...........20 H6
St. Baruch Close................25 A3
St. Benedict Crescent 9 A3
St. Bleddians Close 34 F6
St. Bran Court....................26 E3
St. Brides Close.................14 F5
St. Brides Road 13 A1
St. Brides Way 23 C5
St. Brigid Road 9 A1
St. Brioc Road 9 B1
St. Cadoc Road 9 B2
St. Cadocs Avenue............25 A3
St. Cadocs Rise 24 F5
St. Catherines Court..........23 C5
St. Catherines Mews..........15 D2
St. Cenydd Road 9 B1
St. Clair Court 9 B1
St. Clements Court..............4 E4
St. Curgis Close 28 E4
St. Cyres Close 25 D1

St. Cyres Road...............25 D1
St. Davids Avenue (Dinas Powys)
.................................25 B1
St. Davids Avenue (Llantwit
Major)..................35 D5
St. Davids Court...........17 A6
St. Davids Crescent (Ely)....14 G4
St. Davids Crescent (Murch)
.................................25 D2
St. Davids Road............8 F3
St. Davids Walk..............18 G4
St. Denis Road...............9 B1
St. Dogmaels Avenue.........3 B6
St. Donats Close............25 B2
St. Donats Court.............14 F5
St. Donats Road............16 E5
St. Dyfrig Close...........25 A2
St. Dyfrig Road...............26 F3
St. Edeyrns Close...........10 F1
St. Edeyrns Road...........10 E1
St. Edwens Gardens............9 A2
St. Fagan's Avenue...........30 E1
St. Fagan's Close...........14 H2
St. Fagan's Court............13 D4
St. Fagan's Drive..........13 D1
St. Fagan's Rise..............14 F1
St. Fagan's Road.....14 F2/15 A2
St. Fagan's Street............20 F1
St. Francis Road...............8 F2
St. Garmon Road............26 F3
St. Georges House..........23 D4
St. Georges Road...............9 A3
St. Gildas Road...............9 B1
St. Govans Close............23 B5
St. Gowan Avenue.............9 A2
St. Gwynnos Close..........25 A2
St. Helens Road...............9 A3
St. Illtyd Close...........25 A2
St. Ina Road.....................9 B1
St. Isan Road....................9 B2
St. James Court.............26 E2
St. James Crescent........29 C2
St. John Street................18 F4
St. Johns Close............34 G4
St. Johns Crescent (Canton)
.................................15 D4
St. Johns Crescent (Whitchurch)
...................................8 E1
St. Johns Lane 20 H6
St. Johns Place (Rhoose)...27 B4
St. Johns Place (Whitchurch)8 E1
St. Julian Close............24 F6
St. Lukes Avenue...........26 E3
St. Lythan Close...........25 A3
St. Lythan Court..............14 F5
St. Malo Road...................9 B1
St. Margarets Close..........8 E1
St. Margarets Crescent 17 B1
St. Margarets Park 14 H3
St. Margarets Place 8 F1
St. Margarets Road 15 D4
St. Marks Avenue 9 A4
St. Marks Gardens 9 A4
St. Marks Road..............26 E3
St. Martins Close.............26 E3
St. Martins Crescent..........3 B6
St. Mary Street...............18 F5
St. Marys Avenue...........30 G2
St. Marys Road................8 E1
St. Marys Well Bay Road...32 H3
St. Mellons Road (Gwent)....6 H6
St. Mellons Road (Lisvane)
...................................4 E2-5 B3
St. Michaels Close.........19 A4
St. Michaels Gardens........23 B5
St. Michaels Road...........15 B1
St. Nicholas Close..........25 A2
St. Nicholas Court (Caerau) 14 F5
St. Nicholas Court (Pentwyn)4 G5
St. Nicholas Road............29 D4
St. Ostyn Court.............29 D4
St. Oswalds Road...........24 E6
St. Pauls Avenue (Barry)...30 E3

St. Pauls Avenue (Penarth).26 E3
St. Peters Road..............26 E3
St. Peters Street............17 A2
St. Pierre Close................6 F5
St. Quentins Close.........34 G4
St. Quentins Hill 34 G5
St. Tanwg Road.................9 A2
St. Teilo Avenue 30 F1
St. Teilo Close...............25 B2
St. Teilos Court.............17 C1
St. Winifreds Close........25 A3
Stacey Court...................17 B1
Stacey Road (Dinas Powys)25 A1
Stacey Road (Roath).........17 B2
Stadium Close...............20 E2
Stafford Road.................16 F5
Stag Lane.......................35 B5
Staines Street................15 C2
Stallcourt Avenue (Llantwit Major)
.....................................35 C5
Stallcourt Avenue (Roath) ...10 F6
Stallcourt Close (Cowbridge)
.....................................34 G6
Stallcourt Close (Roath)....10 G6
Stanton Way 26 G5
Stanway Place................14 E3
Stanway Road 14 E4
Stanwell Crescent 20 H6
Stanwell Road 26 E2-G1
Star Street....................17 B3
Starling Road.................35 C1
Station Approach (Barry Island)
.....................................30 F1
Station Approach (Penarth) 26 G1
Station Road (Dinas Powys)25 A2
Station Road (Fairwater)....14 H3
Station Road (Llandaff) 8 B3
Station Road (Llanishen).....3 B5
Station Road (Llantwit Major)
.....................................35 B5
Station Road (Penarth) ...26 G2
Station Road (Radyr).........7 B2
Station Road (Rhoose) 27 D5
Station Road East 33 B2
Station Road West 33 B3
Station Street 30 G2
Station Terrace (Centre) ...18 H4
Station Terrace (Ely) 14 H2
Station Terrace (Penarth) ...26 G2
Steep Street.................20 H6
Stella Close 3 B2
Stenhousemuir Place........17 D2
Stephenson Court 17 A2
Stewart Road 27 D5
Stirling Road (Barry).......33 D6
Stirling Road (Michaelston-s-Ely)
.....................................13 D5
Stockland Street 16 F6
Stonechat Close 12 G1
Stoneleigh Court 15 D2
Storrar Place.................18 E1
Storrar Road..................18 E1
Stradling Close (Barry).....29 C1
Stradling Close (Cowbridge)34 F5
Stradling Close (Sully)....32 E2
Stradling Place 35 C5
Stratford Green 24 E5
Strathnairn Street 16 H1
Stuart Close..................20 E2
Stuart Street 21 A1
Sturminster Road 17 C1
Stuttgart Strasse 16 H3
Subway Road..................30 G3
Sudcroft Street 15 D5
Suffolk House................15 D2
Sullivan Close (Llanrumney).5 D6
Sullivan Close (Penarth) ...26 E4
Sully Moors Road....24 H6-31 D2
Sully Place 26 G2
Sully Road.............20 E6-32 G1
Sully Terrace.................26 G3
Sully Terrace Lane..........26 G2
Sully View......................24 G6

Summeral Court.............15 C2
Summerfield Avenue...........9 B5
Summerfield Court............8 F3
Summerfield Place 8 H2
Summerhill Close............6 G6
Summerland Close.........20 E5
Summerland Crescent 20 E5
Summerwood Close..........7 A6
Sumner Close 7 D4
Sun Street.....................17 B3
Sundew Close (Fairwater) 7 C5
Sundew Close (Penarth) 20 E6
Sunningdale Close..........10 E3
Sunnybrook Court 7 B6
Sunnycroft Close 25 B2
Sunnycroft Lane 25 B2
Sunnycroft Rise 25 B2
Surrey Street 15 C3
Sussex Street 16 F5
Sutherland Mansions 8 E1
Swallowhurst Close.........13 C5
Swanage Close.................6 G6
Swanbridge Grove 32 G2
Swanbridge Road 32 G1
Swansea Street 17 C4
Sweldon Close 14 E6
Swift Close.....................3 B2
Swinton Street...............17 C2
Swyn y Mor...................29 B4
Sycamore Close (Llandough)
.....................................20 E5
Sycamore Close (Murch) ...25 A3
Sycamore Crescent 23 C5
Sycamore House (Hollybush Est.)
...................................7 D1
Sycamore Place 14 G1
Sycamore Tree Close 22 H4
Sylvan Close 7 D6
Syon Park Close.............12 F1
Syr Davids Avenue.........15 C2
System Street.................17 B3
T
Taff Close 29 D1
Taff Cottages..................8 E4
Taff Embankment...........16 G6
Taff Meads Embankment ..16 G5
Taff Street (Butetown) 17 A4
Taff Street (Tongwynlais) 1 B4
Taff Terrace 7 B2
Taff Terrace (Grangetown) .20 G1
Taffs Cottages 31 D2
Tair Erw Road..................9 A2
Tal y Bont Road 14 G4
Tal y Garn Street 9 B5
Talbot Place..................16 E3
Talbot Street..................16 E3
Talworth Street 17 A2
Talyfan Close.................34 G3
Tan y Fron.....................29 B4
Tanglewood Close 3 D3
Tangmere Drive 7 C5
Tapley Close..................14 F6
Tarrws Close 33 B2
Tarwick Drive....................5 D6
Taunton Avenue..............11 B2
Taunton Crescent 11 B2
Tavistock Street.............17 A2
Taymuir Road.................17 D1
Teal Street 17 B4
Tealham Drive..................6 G6
Teamans Row 1 A5
Teasel Avenue 20 E6
Tedder Close....................3 B6
Tegfan 15 D3
Tegfan Close 3 B5
Tegruff Court.................23 C5
Teifi Drive....................29 D1
Teifi Place....................14 G4
Teilo Street 15 D2
Telford Street.................16 E4
Templeton Avenue 2 H2-3 B4
Templeton Close 3 B4
Tenby Close 25 C2

Tennyson Road (Barry).......23 B5
Tennyson Road (Penarth) ...20 F6
Tennyson Way 35 C3
Tensing Close 3 C4
Tensing Terrace 30 H1
Tern Close........................6 E5
Tewdrig Close 35 D5
Tewkesbury Place............9 C5
Tewkesbury Street 9 C6
Thackery Crescent 5 B6
Thaw Close....................27 B4
Theobald Road................15 D4
Theodora Street 17 C2
Thesiger Street..............16 H1
Thistle Way 15 B1
Thomas Street 16 F6
Thompson Avenue 15 B2
Thompson Place 15 B2
Thompson Street 30 G2
Thorley Close.................10 E3
Thorn Grove..................26 G4
Thornbury Close...............8 H1
Thornby Court................17 A5
Thornhill Court.................2 H5
Thornhill Road..................2 H1
Thornhill Street...............15 C3
Thornwood Close..............3 B2
Three Arches Avenue ..3 C6-9 C1
Thrush Close....................6 C6
Tidenham Road..............14 G5
Timbers Square..............17 B1
Timothy Rees Close..........7 C4
Tin Street......................17 B3
Tintagel Close...................3 A3
Tintern Street................15 C3
Titian Road....................17 B4
Tiverton Drive................11 A3
Toftingall Avenue..............8 H2
Tolgate Close 20 E2
Ton yr Ywen Avenue..........9 A1
Topaz Street.................17 B3
Torbay Terrace......27 D5-28 E5
Tordoff Street................30 F1
Torrens Drive..................9 D3
Torrington Road...............5 C6
Tower Hill 26 G2
Tower Way 31 C1
Town Hall Square............34 F4
Town Mill Road...............34 G5
Town Wall.......................18 G4
Towy Road.......................3 C5
Towyn Road 11 C3
Trade Lane.....................16 G5
Trade Street...................16 G5
Trafalgar Road 17 B1
Trebanog Close...............12 E1
Trebanog Crescent..........12 E2
Trebeferad.....................35 D3
Treborth Road................12 E2
Trecastle Avenue..............3 B4
Trechard Drive..................3 B6
Trecynon Road...............12 E2
Tredegar Court................4 B4
Tredegar Street..............18 H5
Tredelerch Road.............11 A5
Tredogan Road...............28 E1
Treetops Close.................7 A6
Trefasser Crescent.....11 D1-12 E1
Tregaron Road................14 E3
Treharne Road.................23 D5
Treharris Street..............17 A2
Treherbert Street.............16 G1
Treherne Drive (Michaelston-s-
Ely)..............................13 C5
Trelai Court...................14 F6
Trelawney Avenue...........11 B4
Trelawney Crescent 11 B4
Trem y Don....................20 E5
Tremadoc Walk...............12 E2
Trenewydd Road.............12 E2
Treoda Court..................11 B4
Treorchy Street...............16 G1
Tresigin Road.................12 E1

Tresilian Close................35 C5
Tresillian Terrace.............16 H5
Tresillian Way.................16 H5
Trevelyan Court..............35 B4
Trevethick Street.............16 E4
Trewartha Court................8 F2
Trinity Street (Barry)........30 E2
Trinity Street (Centre)........18 G5
Triscombe Drive................7 D6
Tristram Close...................2 H3
Troed y Rhiw....................2 E4
Trowbridge Green...........12 E1
Trowbridge Road....11 D2-12 E4
Tudor Close (Fairwater) 14 G2
Tudor Close (Penarth) 26 G4
Tudor Lane.....................16 F5
Tudor Place...................35 C5
Tudor Street...................16 F4
Tudors, The...................10 F6
Tulloch Street.................10 E6
Tummel Close.................10 E2
Turberville Place.............15 D3
Turkey Street..................35 B6
Turner Road...................11 C3
Turnham Green...............10 G5
Turnpike Close...............19 B6
Tuscan Close.................20 E4
Tweedsmuir Road............17 D2
Twyn y Fedwen Road........8 H3
Twyncyn Road................24 H2
Ty Cefn Road.................14 G3
Ty Cerrig (Barry).............23 D6
Ty Cerrig (Pentwyn)...........4 G5
Ty Coch Road.................14 F3
Ty Dewi Sant..................26 E2
Ty Draw Place................10 E5
Ty Draw Road (Lisvane).....10 F4
Ty Draw Road (Roath) 9 D5-10 E5
Ty Dyfan House..............23 C5
Ty Fry Avenue................11 B4
Ty Fry Close...................11 B4
Ty Fry Gardens..............11 B4
Ty Fry Road...................11 B4
Ty Glas Avenue................3 A5
Ty Glas Road.........2 H6-3 B5
Ty Gwenfo......................31 A1
Ty Gwyn Avenue............10 E4
Ty Gwyn Crescent..........10 E4
Ty Gwyn Road (Rhiwbina)....2 G6
Ty Gwyn Road (Roath)....10 E4
Ty Mawr Avenue.............11 A5
Ty Mawr Close................11 A4
Ty Mawr Road (Rumney)...11 A4
Ty Mawr Road (Whitchurch)
.....................................7 D2/8 E4
Ty Nant Road 1 A4
Ty Newydd Road.............30 F1
Ty Parc Close...................7 C4
Ty Pica Drive..................33 B2
Ty Rhiw...........................1 A1
Ty To Maen Close.............5 D5
Ty Wedal.........................9 C3
Ty Wern Avenue................8 H1
Ty Wern Road..................8 H1
Tydfil Place......................9 D5
Tydfil Street...................30 H1
Tyla Lane..................6 G1-G3
Tyla Rhosyr....................34 F6
Tyla Teg..........................2 E5
Tyle House Court............35 A3
Tyler Street...................17 C1
Tymynydd Close................1 A6
Tyn y Cae Grove...............8 G1
Tyn y Coed Lane...............9 D6
Tyn y Coed Place.............9 D6
Tyn y Parc Road........8 F2-G1
Tyn y Pwll Road................8 F2
Tynant 17 A4
Tynant Street..................16 F6
Tyndall Street........17 A4/18 H6
Tyneside Road................21 B1
Tynewydd (Castleton).........6 H2

Tynewydd (Whitchurch).........8 F3
Tynewydd House 30 G2
Tyr Winch Road 5 D4-D6
Tyr y Sarn Road 11 B4
Tyrwhitt Crescent 9 C2

U
Ullswater Avenue 9 D4
Underhill Mansions............8 E1
Universal Street 16 F5
University Place 17 C3
Uphill Close............32 F1
Uphill Road 11 B1
Uplands Crescent.........20 E5
Uplands Road............11 A5
Uplands, The 7 A1
Upper Cliff Close 21 A6
Upper Cliff Drive 21 A6
Upper Clifton Street.........17 B2
Upper Cosmeston Farm....26 F6
Upper Kincraig Street......17 A1
Upper Meadow...........14 E6
Upper Tyn y Parc Terrace ...8 G1
Usk Court............8 F1
Usk Road............3 C5
Usk Way...........29 D1
Uskley Court...........12 E1

V
Vachell Court............35 B4
Vachell Road 14 F4
Vaindre Close 6 F5
Vaindre Drive 6 F5
Vaindre Lane 6 E5/G5
Valarian Close...........12 G1
Vale Court............25 B2
Vale Road...........17 C2
Vale Street...........29 D3
Vale View Close 20 E5
Vale View Crescent 20 E5
Van Street...........16 F6
Vaughan Avenue 15 A1
Velindre Court............8 E2
Velindre Place 8 E2
Velindre Road 7 D2-8 E2
Vendre Close 6 G4
Ventnor Place............9 A4
Venwood Close 33 B3
Verbena Close 6 G5
Vere Street (Cadoxton) 31 A1
Vere Street (Roath) 17 A2
Verlands Close 15 B1
Verlands, The 34 F5
Verlon Close...........24 G6
Verona Place 24 E5
Viaduct Road...........30 H3
Victoria Avenue (Canton) ...15 B2
Victoria Avenue (Penarth) ..26 F1
Victoria Court 10 E6/17 A1
Victoria Park Road........24 E6
Victoria Park Road East...15 B3
Victoria Park Road West...15 B2
Victoria Place 18 G5
Victoria Road (Barry).......29 C4
Victoria Road (Penarth) 26 F3
Victoria Road (Whitchurch) ...8 F2
Victoria Square...........15 C4
Viking Place...........21 D1
Vincent Close...........24 F5
Vincent Court.............14 H3
Vincent Road...........14 H3
Violet Place 8 H3
Violet Row...........16 H1
Virgil Street...........16 E6
Vishwell Road (Cadoxton)..15 C2
Vishwell Road (Wenvoe)
................23 C1/33 B4
Vista Court...........20 H6
Vista Rise 7 C5
Voss Park Close..........35 C3
Voss Park Drive 35 C4

W
Wagtail Road...........35 B1
Walk Farm Drive 6 H1
Walk, The (Plasnewydd)...17 A2

Walk, The (Rumney) 11 A4
Walker Road (Barry)...........30 F1
Walker Road (Ocean Park).17 C4
Walnut Tree Close 22 H3
Walpole Close 5 C5
Walston Close 33 B2
Walston Road 33 B2
Walton Place 16 E6
Wanderers Crescent......13 D4
Warren Evans Court........8 F2
Warwick House 16 E4
Warwick Place 16 F6
Warwick Street 16 F5
Warwick Way...........30 G1
Wasdale Close 10 E5
Washford Avenue...........5 C6
Washington Flats 26 G1
Watchet Close 11 B2
Water Avens Close 12 G1
Waterford Close 16 E5
Waterhall Road 7 C6
Waterhouse Drive...........16 E6
Waterloo Close 10 G6
Waterloo Gardens 17 B1
Waterloo Road 10 F5/F6
Waterston Court...........8 G5
Waterston Road 8 G5
Watford Road...........17 C1
Watson Road...........8 F5
Watson Street...........30 G2
Watton Close 3 B5
Waun Fach...........4 G6
Waun Fawr Road...........8 H1
Waun Gron Road 14 H2-15 A2
Waun Lee Court...........4 G5
Waun y Groes Avenue.....2 H6
Waun y Groes Road 2 H6
Wauntreoda Road 8 H3
Wavell Close 9 C1
Waverley Close 20 E4
Waycock Cross 29 B1
Waycock Road 29 B1/33 A6
Wayside Cottages 19 D6
Wedal Road...........9 C4
Wedmore Road 16 F6
Weekes Close 5 C6
Welby Road...........15 D4
Welford Street...........29 D4
Well Walk...........29 D5
Well Wood...........10 G4
Well Wood Drive...........25 A3
Wellfield Court...........16 E4
Wellfield Place (Canton) ...15 D4
Wellfield Place (Roath)...10 E6
Wellfield Road...........10 E6
Wellington Court...........16 E4
Wellington Street (Riverside)
................16 E4
Wellington Street (Tongwynlais)
................1 B4
Wells Street...........16 E4
Wellwright Road 14 G2
Welwyn Road...........8 H2
Wembley Road...........15 C4
Wenallt Court...........2 G5
Wentloog Close 11 B4
Wentloog Road 11 B4-12 F4
Wentworth Close 6 F5
Wentworth Lane 6 F5
Wenvoe Close 33 B3
Wenvoe Court...........14 F5
Wenvoe Terrace...........30 E3
Werfa Street...........10 E6
Wern Fawr Close...........6 E5
Wern Fawr Lane 5 D5-6 E5
Wern Goch...........10 E1
Wern Goch East...........10 G1
Wern Goch Road...........10 E1
Wern Goch West...........10 F1
Werngethin Lane 12 E1
Wesley Avenue 27 C4
Wesley Court...........25 A2
Wesley Lane 18 H4

Wesley Street 35 B5
Wessex Place 29 D5
Wessex Street 15 B3
West Acre...........35 A3
West Bute Street 21 A1
West Canal Wharf 18 G6
West Close 21 A1
West End Terrace 35 B6
West Grove (Caerau) 17 A3
West Grove (Plasnewydd) ..16 H2
West Grove Court...........17 A3
West Hill Street 35 B6
West Lee...........16 F3
West Luton Place 17 A3
West Orchard Crescent ...15 A2
West Rise 3 C4
West Road (Barry) 31 C1
West Road (Llandaff North) ..7 D4
West Street...........35 B6
West Terrace 26 F1
West View...........1 A1
West Walk...........30 E1
West Wharf Road...........16 H5
Westbourne Court (Cadoxton)
................24 E5
Westbourne Court(Rumney)
................11 C4
Westbourne Crescent 7 D3
Westbourne Road (Llandaff North)
................7 D3-8 E2
Westbourne Road (Penarth)
................26 G2
Westbury Close 23 D6
Westbury Terrace...........15 C2
Western Avenue........8 G6-15 A2
Western Avenue Court......15 A2
Western Avenue North......8 H6
Western Drive 8 G6
Westfield Avenue 8 H2
Westfield Road...........8 G3
Westgate...........34 F5
Westgate Square 18 F5
Westgate Street 18 F4
Westminster Crescent 4 E6
Westminster Drive (Cyncoed)4 E5
Westminster Drive (Sully)...32 F2
Westmorland Street 15 D4
Weston Avenue 32 F2
Weston Road 11 B2
Weston Square...........31 A1
Weston Street...........31 A1
Westonbirt Close 12 E1
Westra...........24 F3
Westra Court...........15 C2
Westville Road...........10 F6
Westville Walk...........10 E6
Westward Rise 29 B4
Westwood Court...........26 G1
Wharf Street 16 H5/18 G6
Wharfdale Road 4 H5
Wharton Close 27 C5
Wharton Street...........18 G5
Wheatley Road...........14 F4
Whinchat Close 6 G6
Whitaker Road...........18 E1
Whitchurch Place 9 C6
Whitchurch Road...........9 B4
Whitcliffe Drive 26 G5
White Barn Road...........2 H5
White House...........29 D5
White House Close 35 C6
Whiteacre Close 3 B3
Whitefield Road 8 F5
Whitehall Avenue 11 A4
Whitehall Close 33 B2
Whitehall Parade 11 A4
Whitehall Place 11 A4
Whitehall Road 8 E5
Whiteoaks Drive 5 D5
Whitesands Road...........2 H4
Whiteways...........35 B4
Whitewell Drive...........35 D5
Whitewell Road 23 A5

Whitland Close 7 C6
Whitland Crescent 7 C6
Whitmuir Road 17 D2
Whitton Close...........27 B4
Whittle Road...........15 D6
Whitworth Court...........16 F5
Wick Road 35 B6
Wicken Close 6 G6
Widecombe Drive 11 A4
Wigmore Close...........3 B3
Wild Gardens Road...........9 D2
Wilfred Brook House 20 F1
Wilfrid Street...........30 H1
William Street 15 D2
Williams Crescent 30 F2
Williams Way 16 G6
Williton Road 5 C6
Willow Close 26 E2
Willow Court...........17 A2
Willow Crescent 23 C6
Willow Dale Close...........14 F1
Willow Dale Road...........14 E1
Willow Grove...........6 F5
Willow Walk...........34 F4
Willowbrook Drive 6 G6-12G1
Willowdene Way 6 F5
Willowfield Court...........10 E1
Willowherb Close 12 G1
Willowmere...........20 E4
Willowood...........10 G3
Willows Avenue...........17 D3
Willows, The 8 F2
Willowtree Close 22 H4
Wilson Place...........14 F5
Wilson Road 14 E3-F5
Wilson Street...........17 C2
Wimborne Close...........35 D5
Wimborne Road...........31 A3
Wimbourne Crescent...........32 F2
Winchester Avenue 10 F5
Winchester Close...........30 E2
Windermere Avenue...........9 C3
Windflower Close 6 F6
Windhover Close...........12 G1
Windmill Close...........3 B3
Windmill Court...........35 B5
Windmill La. (Cowbridge)...34 G4
Windmill La.(Llantwit Major) 35 B5
Windrush Place...........14 G1
Windsor Arcade 26 G1
Windsor Avenue 7 A1
Windsor Close (Llantwit Major)
................35 B4
Windsor Close (Radyr)...........7 A1
Windsor Court...........26 H2
Windsor Crescent...........7 B2
Windsor Esplanade 20 H2
Windsor Gardens 14 H3
Windsor Green 14 H3
Windsor House 16 G4
Windsor La. (Centre) 16 H3/18 H4
Windsor La. (Penarth)...........20 G6
Windsor Mews...........17 A4
Windsor Place (Centre)...........16 H3
Windsor Place (Penarth)...26 F1
Windsor Road (Barry) 29 D3
Windsor Road (Penarth)...20 F5
Windsor Road (Radyr) 7 A2
Windsor Road (Splott)...17 A4
Windsor Terrace (Butetown)20 H2
Windsor Terrace (Penarth).26 G1
Windsor Terrace Lane 26 G1
Windway Avenue...........15 A2
Windway Road...........15 A2
Windy Ridge...........25 C2
Wine Street...........35 B6
Wingate Drive 9 C1
Wingfield Road...........8 E3
Winifred Place 23 B5
Winnipeg Drive...........10 E2
Winston Road...........23 A5
Winston Square 23 A5

Withycombe Road...........5 C5
Witla Court Road...........11 C2
Wolfe Close (Cadoxton) 24 F5
Wolffe Close (Cowbridge)...34 G6
Wolfs Castle Avenue...........3 B4
Womanby Street...........18 F4
Wood Close 3 D4
Wood Cottages...........1 A1
Wood Street (Centre) 18 F6
Wood Street (Penarth) 26 F1
Woodcock Street 17 A2
Woodfield Avenue 7 B3
Woodford Close 7 D6
Woodham Close...........30 E1
Woodham Park...........30 E1
Woodham Road...........30 H3
Woodland Crescent...........10 E3
Woodland Place (Penarth) ..26 F1
Woodland Place (Roath)...17 A2
Woodland Road...........17 A2
Woodlands Close 34 F3
Woodlands Cottages...........19 C1
Woodlands Court...........30 F2
Woodlands Park Drive...........14 F6
Woodlands Road...........30 F2
Woodlands, The 3 D3
Woodlawn Way 3 A2
Woodpecker Square 35 C1
Woodside Court...........3 D4
Woodstock...........11 D2
Woodstock Close 29 D2
Woodvale Avenue...........4 F6
Woodville Road...........9 D6/16 G1
Woolacombe Avenue...........11 C1
Woolaston Avenue 9 D2-10 E2
Woolmer Close...........7 C5
Worcester Court...........20 F1
Wordsworth Av. (Penarth)...26 E1
Wordsworth Av. (Roath)...17 A2
Wordsworth Close...........35 C4
Working Street...........18 G4
Worle Avenue 11 B2
Worle Place...........11 B2
Wren Close 12 F1
Wren Road 35 B1
Wrengethin Lane 12 F1
Wrexham Court...........11 D2
Wroughton Place...........14 H2
Wye Close...........29 C1
Wyeverne Court...........16 H1
Wyeverne Road...........16 G1
Wyfan Place...........9 A5
Wyncliffe Road 5 A5
Wynd Street...........30 H1
Wyndham Arcade...........18 G6
Wyndham Crescent...........16 E3
Wyndham Place 16 E4
Wyndham Road...........16 E3
Wyndham Street (Barry) 30 G2
Wyndham Street (Riverside)16 E4
Wyndham Street (Tongwynlais)
................1 B4
Wyndham Terrace...........3 C5
Wynnstay Close 16 E6
Wyon Close...........7 C4

Y
Y Goedwig...........2 F5
Y Groes...........2 G6
Yew Tree Court (Barry) 29 D4
Yew Tree Court (Penarth) ...10 E5
Yewtree Close 14 F1
Ynysfach Yard...........1 A4
Yorath Road...........8 G2
York Court...........17 A5
York Mansions...........8 E1
York Place (Barry) 29 D3
York Place (Grangetown)...20 F2
York Street 15 C3
Youldon House...........25 B2
Ystrad Close 6 F6
Ystrad Street...........16 G6

Z
Zinc Street...........17 B3